Confident Computing for
the Over 50s

D0514069

Confident Computing for the Over 50s

Bob Reeves

For UK order enquiries: please contact Bookpoint Ltd, 130 Milton Park, Abingdon, Oxon OX14 4SB. Telephone: +44 (0) 1235 827720. Fax: +44 (0) 1235 400454. Lines are open 09.00–17.00, Monday to Saturday, with a 24-hour message answering service. Details about our titles and how to order are available at www.teachyourself.com

For USA order enquiries: please contact McGraw-Hill Customer Services, PO Box 545, Blacklick, OH 43004-0545, USA. Telephone: 1-800-722-4726. Fax: 1-614-755-5645.

For Canada order enquiries: please contact McGraw-Hill Ryerson Ltd, 300 Water St, Whitby, Ontario L1N 9B6, Canada. Telephone: 905 430 5000. Fax: 905 430 5020.

Long renowned as the authoritative source for self-guided learning – with more than 50 million copies sold worldwide – the Teach Yourself series includes over 500 titles in the fields of languages, crafts, hobbies, business, computing and education.

British Library Cataloguing in Publication Data: a catalogue record for this title is available from the British Library.

Library of Congress Catalog Card Number: on file.

First published in UK 2009 by Hodder Education, part of Hachette UK, 338 Euston Road, London NW1 3BH.

First published in US 2009 by The McGraw-Hill Companies, Inc.

This edition published 2010.

Previously published as Teach Yourself Computing for the Over 50s

The Teach Yourself name is a registered trade mark of Hodder Headline.

Copyright © Bob Reeves 2010

Typeset by MPS Limited, a Macmillan company.

Printed in Great Britain for Hodder Education, an Hachette UK Company, 338 Euston Road, London NW1 3BH, by CPI Cox & Wyman, Reading, Berkshire RG1 8EX.

The publisher has used its best endeavours to ensure that the URLs for external websites referred to in this book are correct and active at the time of going to press. However, the publisher and the author have no responsibility for the websites and can make no guarantee that a site will remain live or that the content will remain relevant, decent or appropriate.

Hachette UK's policy is to use papers that are natural, renewable and recyclable products and made from wood grown in sustainable forests. The logging and manufacturing processes are expected to conform to the environmental regulations of the country of origin.

Impression number   10 9 8 7 6 5 4 3 2 1
Year   2014 2013 2012 2011 2010

Contents

Welcome to Confident Computing for the Over 50s!

I've written this book specifically for the more mature newcomer to computers. It covers a comprehensive range of typical computer uses and assumes that you have no prior knowledge of using a computer. I've tried to keep jargon to a minimum. Where I have had to use any, the word is explained and you will find it in the jargon-busting glossary at the back of the book.

Throughout this book, when you need to click on something on the screen, it will be shown in the text in single speech marks. For example, if you need to click on a menu on the screen called Save, the instruction will read: Click 'Save'. When you need to press one of the keys on the keyboard, the name of that key will be shown in capitals. For example, if you need to press the ENTER key, the instructions will read: Press ENTER.

I would recommend that you work through the chapters in order, although you can dip in and out. Some chapters are best read together. In particular:

▶ *Chapters 1–5 cover all of the basics*
▶ *Chapters 6 and 7 cover word processing (typing documents)*
▶ *Chapters 8 and 9 cover email*
▶ *Chapters 10–16 cover the Internet*

- ▶ *Chapters 17 and 18 cover digital photography*
- ▶ *Chapters 19 and 20 cover how to create safe copies of your work*
- ▶ *Chapters 21–23 cover the creation of various publications (e.g. posters, leaflets, etc.) using desktop publishing software*
- ▶ *Chapters 24 and 25 cover the use of spreadsheets for working with numerical or financial information*
- ▶ *Chapter 26 covers the creation of a database*
- ▶ *Chapter 27 covers the presentation of a slideshow*

The intention of the book is to build up an arsenal of skills using a range of different computer programs. You will soon discover that skills learned in one aspect of computing can be transferred to others. There are hints and tips throughout the chapters to help you on your way.

The book features examples from the most common programs being used at present including Microsoft® Word, PowerPoint, Excel, Access and Publisher. Several other programs are used, many of which are freely available from the Internet.

One of the problems with computers is that the programs are changing all the time. When changes are made, a new 'version' is brought out. Therefore, there are lots of different versions of the same programs available. The good news is that this does not fundamentally change the way in which the program works. However, it does mean that some of the screens might look a bit different. This book uses Windows® 7 and Microsoft® Office 2007.

Finally, when you first start, computers can be a bit scary. One mature evening-class student commented that the computer screen is so cluttered it looks like a flight deck on an aeroplane with little buttons and signs all over the place. However, the big difference is that if you go wrong on the computer, it doesn't matter. Your computer is virtually impossible to break – so don't be scared of it, just click away and see what happens. Have fun.

Bob Reeves
2010

About the author

Bob Reeves has been working with computers for the last 25 years. He started his career in one of the country's leading financial services companies involved in IT and training roles.

He later retrained as a teacher specializing in business and ICT. He has taught thousands of children and adults on a range of business and ICT courses over the years with students as young as 4 and as old as 80.

He has worked on a number of projects here and abroad related to computer education and has written for a number of computer publications. He has written several textbooks on ICT including 'Internet and Email for the Over 50s' also available in the Teach Yourself series.

Bob is married with two grown-up sons. His wife has been his most difficult student to date and his two sons both chose careers that had nothing to do with computers.

Only got one minute?

There's been something of a computing revolution going on in the last 20 years. If you've picked this book up, it's probably because you want to join the revolution! There has never been a better time.

The first thing that most computer users have to do is go out and buy and computer and then come home and switch it on. This can be a daunting prospect if you've never done it before.

You might hear words like 'hardware' and 'software' and talk of gigahertz and gigabytes. Hardware refers to all the physical bits that you can touch like the screen, keyboard and the computer itself. Software or 'programs' are all the things you use your computer for like word-processing for typing letters and documents and emailing for sending each other messages. And as for the giga-thing, the bigger the number the better!

The basics of computing are quite simple. You use the mouse to point and click at things on the screen and you use the keyboard to type stuff in. You can master these basics by working through the brief introduction to Word, which is Microsoft's word-processing software.

The basics of Internet and email are also relatively simple. A few carefully chosen words typed into Google and the ability to spot a link on a web page (the pointer changes shape!) and you will be 'surfing the net' and accessing the billions of pages of information that are out there.

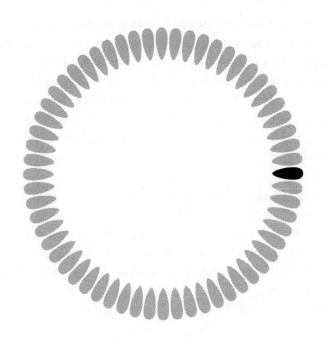

5 Only got five minutes?

In a world full of computer whizz kids, it's easy to forget that anyone over the age of about 40 did not receive any formal education in computers and IT when they were at school. According to the latest figures, over 70% of households in the UK now own a computer so there has clearly been something of a revolution going on over the last few years. At the same time there has been the phenomenon of email and the World Wide Web, which now has an estimated 1 billion users around the world, 50 million of them in the UK.

Computers, once the domain of the 'nerds', are for everyone. That's not to say that they are easy to use, but they are much easier now than they have ever been. Computers can at first appear to be illogical and confusing. There some truth in this. A case in point is that you don't actually switch the computer off using the on/off switch, but more on that later!

When you switch the computer on it whirrs away for a minute or two before you are faced with a screen with lots of little pictures on it. This screen is called your desktop and the little images are called icons. Think of this like a normal desktop – a flat surface with lots of things on it that you might do.

You use the mouse the move a pointer on the screen. When the pointer is over one of the icons you press the left mouse button twice (a 'double click') and something happens. The icons usually link to software, also known as applications or programs. These are all the things that we use our computers for. There is a program for getting on the Internet, one for emails, one for typing documents and so on.

When a program opens, we are faced with a set of options. These are not as daunting as they may appear at first. In fact, very few people use all of the options available in any program so you don't need to know what all of them are. Also, many of the features in one program are the same in other programs too.

If you take Microsoft Word for example, there are options to save, print and open, which are common to all Microsoft programs. Typing text into Word is the same as it typing text into any other program. What this means is that you quickly build up an arsenal of skills that you can transfer from one program to another. Once you can type a letter in Word, you can also type an email.

'Surfing the net' is another one of those phrases that you hear banded about. There are billions of web pages full of information but the key to accessing all of this information is actually quite simple. Using web browser software such as Internet Explorer, which you will already have on your computer, you can access a 'search engine' such as Google. Using a few carefully chosen search words you can very quickly find what you are looking for.

Websites are a collection of individual web pages. Once you are inside a website you will find that there are common ways of moving around so that you can access even more information. Web pages are linked together using 'hyperlinks'. You will know when you are on a hyperlink because the mouse pointer changes shape. When you click on the link it will take you off to another page, where you may find other links to follow and so on and so on.

Within a few clicks you will be 'multi-tasking' (computing allegedly has more jargon than any other subject) which simply means that you will be doing more than one thing at the same time. Windows is geared up to let you have several tasks on the go all at the same time and to flip between these tasks effortlessly. This means that you can be working on your great unfinished novel and take the odd break to email your friends or surf the Internet.

And when you have had enough and it's time to switch off, you click on the 'Start' icon in the bottom left hand corner of the screen, which you will soon become familiar with, and you can shut down before you start all over again.

1

Choosing a computer

In this chapter you will learn
- *what the main parts of the computer are*
- *how to understand a computer specification*
- *what specification of computer you need for the things you will be using your computer for*
- *whether to have a laptop or a desktop computer*
- *how to make your decision of what to buy and where to buy it*

1.1 What do you want to use your computer for?

You might not know the answer to this question yet! However, you may already know what you are not going to use your computer for and this might help you in your choice. The price of the computer is usually based on how fast it works and how much information you want to keep on it.

When you buy a computer, the manufacturer will publish the specification of the computer. A basic computer system is made up of the base unit, sometimes called a tower, a screen, keyboard, mouse and printer. Computer equipment such as this is called hardware.

You will also need what is called software. This refers to the programs that you will run on the computer. Programs are needed to let you do all the things you want to do like type letters, send emails and get onto the Internet.

1.2 What you will need

The base unit or tower is where all the clever stuff goes on. The main features to look for when you are choosing your computer are:

Processor

The processor is the brains of the computer. Everything that is done on the computer goes through the processor. The speed is measured in gigahertz (GHz). The simple rule is the higher the number of GHz, the faster your computer will work. Anything over 2 GHz is perfectly adequate for most computer users.

Memory

This is sometimes called RAM (random access memory). This is measured in gigabtyes (GB). The simple rule here is the higher the number of GB, the faster your computer will run. 2 GB of memory is the minimum recommended when running Windows 7 – more is better.

Hints and tips

How important is speed? All modern computers are fast. Most things you do on the computer such as typing documents, surfing the Internet, emailing, etc. do not require a really fast processor or lots of memory. If you plan to use your computer for playing computer games or editing movies, then faster processor speeds and more memory might be needed.

Hard disk drive (HDD)

This is the amount of information that the computer can store. This is measured in gigabtyes (GB) and, you guessed it – the bigger the number, the more information it will store. Anything over 100 GB is more than adequate for most computer users.

CD or DVD drive

These are the trays on the front of the tower that slide out so that you can put in a CD or DVD. CDs and DVDs have all sorts of information on them including computer programs, data and films. It is recommended that you get a DVD drive as these will cope with CDs and DVDs. A CD drive will cope only with CDs. It is recommended to get a DVD-R or DVD RW, which means you can save information onto DVDs as well as take information off them.

Hints and tips

Computer manufacturers bring out new computers all the time. They are always bringing out faster processors and increased memory. This means that your computer will start to become out of date quite quickly. This does not really matter for most users.

Monitor

This is the screen on which everything is displayed. As with the computer tower, there are thousands of variations to choose from. All new monitors now are flat, which means that they take up only a small amount of space on your desk. The main decision is about the size of the screen. The size is measured in inches. Standard sizes are from 15 to 19 inches. Bigger screens are more expensive but are much easier to read. The best advice is to go to a shop and have a look at the different sizes.

Keyboard and mouse

You don't usually get much choice with these as your computer will come with a standard keyboard and mouse. All keyboards are pretty much the same and you use them for typing in letters and numbers. The mouse is a pointing device. You point at things on the screen and click the buttons to make things happen. If you don't like wires everywhere, you can invest in a wireless mouse.

Hints and tips

Almost every keyboard is a QWERTY keyboard. This is from the layout of the letters on the keyboard – the first six letters starting from the top left spell QWERTY. This layout is exactly the same as on typewriters.

Printer

This is for producing printed copies of anything you do on your computer. As with everything else to do with computers, there are thousands to choose from. The main decisions are whether you want an inkjet or a laser printer and whether you want colour or just black and white prints. Inkjets are usually cheaper to buy, but the ink cartridges can run out quickly and are expensive to replace. Laser printers are slightly more expensive to buy, produce slightly better quality and print more quickly.

Colour printing is more expensive than black and white printing as you have to buy colour cartridges as well as black ones. However, unless the only thing you will be doing is typing documents, then a colour printer is going to be essential.

An inkjet printer.

1.3 The operating system (Windows 7)

You will also need to choose what software you want. When you buy your hardware, you usually get some software with it. There is more on this in Chapter 3, but at this stage you must make sure that the computer you buy comes with an operating system. This is a program that enables your computer to work and is essential. The most common operating system is Microsoft Windows®, which normally comes as part of the price of the computer. Make sure any computer you choose has this on it already.

Hints and tips

Several different versions of Windows have appeared over time. Most new computers come with Windows 7 Home Premium or Professional. Either of these is fine.

1.4 Plugging things in using USB ports

In the next chapter, you will learn about a range of additional devices that can be plugged into your computer. Most of these devices attach using a USB connection. Make sure your computer has got at least six USB ports. This will allow up to six different devices to be plugged in at the same time.

USB ports.

1.5 Connecting to the Internet

If you want to connect to the Internet you will need a
modem or router. This is a device that might be built
into the computer, or may be plugged into the back.
You have to choose which company to get your Internet
connection from, for example Tiscali, BT, AOL, etc.
and they will normally supply you with a modem or
router to plug into one of the USB ports. The other end
plugs into the telephone socket. If you have broadband,
you will also be supplied with filters, which you need to
plug into those other phone sockets to which telephones
will be attached. These enable you to make phone calls
while using the Internet at the same time.

You might like to consider have a wireless router.
As the name suggests, this means that you do not have
to physically plug your computer in as the information
will travel wirelessly. Your Internet access will be a bit
slower than plugging in with a wire but it does mean
that you can have your computer anywhere in the
house and you will still be able to get access to the
Internet without having to trail wire around all over
the place.

These days, broadband is available in most areas.
Broadband means that the access to all of the information
is quite quick. Without broadband, access is boringly
slow.

A wireless routes.

1.6 Laptop or desktop?

The computers discussed so far relate to desktop computers. As the name suggests, these are computers that you keep in one place (on your desk) at home. In the examples before, you would put your tower unit on, or under your desk.

Another option is to go portable and get a laptop. Laptops have all the same bits as a desktop, but they are all put together into one portable unit. The keyboard, mouse and screen are all part of the laptop contained within the casing. Laptops are light, portable and run for about four hours on batteries. You can plug them in and recharge them at home or even on trains these days.

You can do exactly the same thing with a laptop as with a desktop. So, should you get one? On the plus side, they are portable, take up less space in your house, can be used anywhere and do everything a desktop can do. On the downside, they are slightly more expensive to buy, more easily lost or stolen and some people don't like the smaller keyboards and screens that they tend to have. It is largely a matter of personal choice.

1.7 Where to get your computer from

As you will discover when you try to buy a computer, there are several different manufacturers to choose from and you can buy from a range of places. Generally speaking, you get what you pay for and it pays to shop around.

- *High Street chains: These are quite competitive on price and have a good selection of computers. They are a safe bet if you don't have a good local specialist.*
- *Specialist computer shops: The level of advice you get will probably be a lot better in a specialist computer shop, though they may not be able to be as competitive on price. They are usually good at looking after you if you have any problems later. It's good if you can find one that comes recommended.*
- *The Internet/mail order: You can get some real bargains from catalogues and the Internet (if you have access). Internet and mail order businesses don't have the overheads that the shops do and this is how they can do it cheaper. The disadvantage is that you won't get to see the computer 'in the flesh' before you buy it. Use a bigger company that you have heard of or that has been recommended. You could always find the computer you want in a shop and then see if you can get the same thing cheaper on the Internet.*

Most new computers come with at least one year's warranty although this can be extended to three. Most warranties require the computer to be sent to the manufacturer, which means you will be without it for a week or so.

IMPORTANT THINGS TO REMEMBER FROM THIS CHAPTER

1 *Processor speed is one of the key factors in how fast your computer will work. It is measured in Gigahertz (GHz).*

2 *Memory (or RAM) is another key factor that determines how quickly your computer will work. This is measured in Gigabytes (Gb).*

3 *The hard disk is where all information is stored. This is also measured in Gigabytes (Gb).*

4 *Your computer should have a CD or DVD drive. If choosing just one go for a DVD-RW as this will cope with CDs and DVDs.*

5 *Monitors are measured in inches across the diagonal face. 17–19 inches is common although you might like to pay extra for a bigger one.*

6 *There are two main types of printer: inkjet and laser. You can get these in either mono (black and white) or colour.*

7 *Windows 7 is an operating system. It is a package of software that controls all aspects of the computer.*

8 *If you are buying a computer make sure it has lots of USB ports – at least six if possible.*

9 *You will need a modem or router if you want to get onto the Internet.*

10 *If you are buying a computer, think about where you will be using it as it may be a good idea to get a laptop, which is portable.*

2

Other equipment you might need

In this chapter you will learn
- *what other computer equipment you might need*
- *what specification of equipment is needed*

2.1 What peripherals do you need?

Many of the peripherals that you can buy have quite specific functions, so it is not worth investing in them unless you have good reason to do so. Most devices these days plug into your computer using a USB connection and your computer should have at least six USB ports for you to plug in to.

> **Hints and tips**
> Most devices are now 'plug and play', which means that when you plug them in, the computer spots that they have been plugged in and they will work automatically.

DIGITAL CAMERA

These are now more common than old-fashioned cameras. They do not use film. Instead, they store the image electronically on a card that slots into the camera. You can store hundreds of images on a card and can transfer the images onto your computer where you can store and print them.

The main things to look for when buying a digital camera are:

▶ *Megapixels: This refers to the number of tiny dots used to make up the image. The larger the number of megapixels, the better clarity you get in your finished photographs. Anything over 8 megapixels is adequate for the average photographer.*

▶ *Optical and digital zoom: This refers to the amount of magnification you can get, i.e. how far you can focus in on images that are far away. Optical zoom* is better as it is achieved using the camera's lens; 3.3 optical zoom is usually sufficient. Digital zoom digitally zooms in on the image; 6 digital zoom is perfectly adequate.

▶ LCD: This is the small screen that you use to preview the image. The size is measured in inches; 2.5 inches is adequate although larger screens are easier to see.

Hints and tips

You can also buy digital camcorders, which you can use to record moving images. Like a digital camera, you can transfer the images onto your computer where you can watch the film you have made.

WEB CAM

This is a camera that you place on top of your screen, which takes moving pictures of you! The idea of this is that you can contact people using your computer and they can see and hear you while you are talking to them. If they have a web cam at their end, you can see them too. These are particularly useful if you have friends in other countries that you would like to see and hear, rather than just write to. Choose one that has a resolution of 640 × 480 or higher. The higher the resolution, the clearer the images will be. If you want to be heard, you will need a web cam with a built-in microphone.

A web cam.

SCANNER

A scanner is a device that works a bit like a photocopier. You put the document or picture onto its glass surface

A scanner.

and by scanning it, you create a computerized version of the document or picture. This is particularly useful if you have old photographs that you would like to put onto the computer. Scanners can also be used to scan any other kind of document as long as it is A4 size or less. If you do get a scanner, make sure it has at least 4800dpi. This is dots per inch. The higher the number, the clearer the scanned images will be.

MEMORY STICK

These are small storage devices that let you store information in a portable way. If you ever need to move information from one computer to another, then you will need a memory stick. These are sometimes called flash memory or flash drives. They are very small and plug into the USB port. You can copy information onto them and then take them with you. For example, if you go to an evening class and want to take in some work that you did on your home computer, then you can use a memory stick. The amount that a memory stick can store is measured in gigabytes (GB). The price of these has come down massively over the last few years and a 1 GB stick will only cost you a few pounds so you might as well buy one with lots of memory on it.

A memory stick.

SPEAKERS

These are just the same as the speakers on your stereo or radio except you plug them into the back of your computer. You will need speakers if you want to play music or videos, or if you want to talk to other people over the Internet, for example, using a web cam. Speakers that plug into the electricity supply can deliver more volume if needed, though those that draw their power through the USB ports are often loud enough. The amount of volume you can get is measured in watts (W). More watts mean more volume.

CD/DVD BURNER

This allows you to make your own CDs or DVDs. There are many different formats of CD and DVD. A standard CD or DVD drive will allow you to read information from the disk, but not to put any information back onto it. You might want to be able to create (burn) your own CDs and DVDs. For example, if you take lots of photographs, you could burn them onto a CD to give to family and friends. If you have made a film using a digital camcorder, you might want to burn it onto a DVD. If you think you might want to do this, then you should make sure that you get a CD-R, CD-RW or DVD-R or DVD-RW. The R means recordable and the RW means re-writable. You can buy some that plug into a USB port or you can buy a computer that already has one built into your base unit/tower.

The open tray of a DVD drive.

Hints and tips

Although we tend to associate DVDs with films, they are actually used to store any kind of information (films, music, photographs, documents, etc.). DVDs can store much more information than a CD so it is best to get a DVD drive.

IMPORTANT THINGS TO REMEMBER FROM THIS CHAPTER

1 *'Peripherals' is the general term used for additional devices that you can plug into your computer.*

2 *You can copy images off a digital camera to be stored and viewed on your computer.*

3 *You can connect a web cam, which allows you to send still or moving images of yourself to someone on another computer.*

4 *A scanner can be used to create digitized images of photographs or other paper-based images and documents.*

5 *Memory sticks are small devices that plug into your USB ports and can be used to transfer information from one computer to another.*

6 *Speakers are needed to hear any kind of audio including music or voice, for example, when making a phone call over the Internet.*

7 *If speakers plug into the mains supply, the sound can be amplified much better than if they take their power from the computer.*

8 *If you computer has a CD-R, CD-R, DVD-R or DVD-RW, it is capable of copying information onto CDs and DVDs.*

9 *The R stands for Recordable, which means that information can be recorded onto them but only once.*

10 *The RW stands for Rewritable and means that they can be used over and over again to store information.*

3

Programs (software) you might need

In this chapter you will learn
- *what a computer program is*
- *which computer programs are essential*
- *what computer programs you might need*

3.1 What software do you need?

Software allows you to do the things you want to do. Without software, you can't do anything with your computer – it is just a pile of useless equipment. There are different types of software, each of which allows you to carry out different jobs on your computer. You may have heard of some already. For example: word processing software is needed to type letters and other types of documents; web browser software is needed to access the Internet; email software is needed to send and receive emails.

So what do you need?

Microsoft

Microsoft is the biggest name in standard software. Its owner, Bill Gates, is one of the richest men in the world. Microsoft is responsible for Word, Excel, PowerPoint, Access, Publisher, Internet Explorer, Outlook and Hotmail, which are some of the most common software used. They also make Windows. Now you can see why he's one of the richest men in the world!

Microsoft Office

This is a collection of different bits of software designed to do different jobs. They come together as a bundle, which makes it cheaper than buying them each individually. Although, you might not want all of the software right now, it is better to buy it as a bundle as it will cost much more to buy it individually later on. It is recommended that you buy the latest version of Microsoft® Office. You will get:

▶ *Word: This is word processing software used for typing documents of all types. For example, you can use this for typing letters, minutes, essays, etc.*
▶ *Excel: This is spreadsheet software used for handling numbers and calculations. For example, you can use this if you want to keep financial records on your computer.*
▶ *PowerPoint: This is used to create slideshow presentations. For example, you can use this if you want to make slideshows of your holiday photographs.*
▶ *Access: This is database software used to store records. For example, you could use this to record*

club members or names and addresses of personal friends.

▶ *Publisher: This is desktop publishing software used to create publications of all kinds. For example, you could use this to create posters, flyers or pamphlets.*

▶ *Outlook: This is an email program, with additional personal organizer functions. You can set it up on your computer and send and receive email. However, you may prefer to use one of the free web-based emails referred to later.*

Hints and tips

Microsoft sells different versions of Office. Some of them do not contain all the software listed above. Make sure you get the version you want with the software that you need in it.

Internet Explorer

This is called a browser and is needed to view all of the information on the Internet. Internet Explorer (IE) is usually found on any computer that has Windows on it – so you have probably already got it.

Email

Most email software is web-based. This means that you do not need to buy it as you can use it for free on the Internet. Another advantage of web-based software is that you can use it from anyone's computer – you do not have to use your own. You will get free email from the company that you get your Internet from, known as your Internet Service Provider (ISP).

Internet Service Provider (ISP)

This is a service that gives you access to the Internet. It is basically a telephone service that allows you to get Internet access down your telephone line. This service is provided by a business, e.g. BT, NTL, Talk Talk, etc. To get on the Internet, you must have an ISP. There are lots to choose from and they vary in price and the speed at which they work. It is a competitive business so it is worth shopping around and asking family and friends which one they use and whether they are happy with it. If you live in a cable TV area you can get a deal where TV, telephone and Internet is all available through cable at a fixed price per month.

Anti-virus

This software stops your computer getting infected with computer viruses. Viruses are small programs written by people with nothing better to do. They attack your computer and can damage it or the information that is on it. Anti-virus software searches your computer for viruses and kills them. If you buy anti-virus software you are entitled to updates, which means that you will get new versions of the software that will kill any new viruses.

3.2 Software supplied with devices

Whenever you buy a new device such as a camera or a scanner, it will come with a CD or DVD that contains the software for the device. All devices need software to make them work on your computer. The software also includes useful functions. For example, the software that comes with your digital camera will allow you to browse and edit your photographs on-screen. The problem with these programs is that each one is different. For example, the software supplied with a Canon camera will be different from that supplied with a Kodak camera.

Having said that, most software conforms to some standard rules, as you will see later. All software should also be supplied with a user manual to help you get started.

3.3 Free software

Generally speaking, you get what you pay for and this is also the case with free software! There is a lot of free software available on the Internet for you to download. If you buy a computer magazine, you often get a CD packed with free software. Some of this is genuinely good stuff. For example, software companies often give away older versions of their software to encourage you to buy the latest version. Some free software is free only for 30 days and then you have to buy it – so watch out for this. It will normally run out just after the 30 days without causing any problems. Some free software is free because it's rubbish.

As a rule, it is recommended that you put free software onto your computer only if you think you will be using it. The temptation is to clutter up your computer with all of this stuff because it is free. However, every time you add something to your computer, it does alter the settings, which might cause problems elsewhere. Also, you will end up with a long list of programs making it harder to find the ones you do want to use.

3.4 Licences

Finally, make sure that any free software you use is genuine. It is easy to create copies of software and you may know people who offer you 'free' software. It is usually illegal to use software that you have not paid for. When you buy legitimate software you get a licence to use it on your computer. In theory, you can be fined heavily for using unlicensed software.

Make sure that you keep the original packaging of all software that you buy, as this is the licence. This also means making sure that you get a copy of Windows from whomever sold you your computer.

IMPORTANT THINGS TO REMEMBER FROM THIS CHAPTER

1 *Software is also referred to as 'programs' or 'applications'.*

2 *Software is what you actually use your computer for. For example, you need software to write letters, send email or surf the Internet.*

3 *Microsoft Office is a suite of software that is used to carry out common computer functions.*

4 *There are different versions of Microsoft Office. The 'Home and Student' edition is suitable for most home users and is the cheapest.*

5 *Internet Explorer enables you to get onto the Internet. You will also need an Internet Service Provider (ISP) to provide you with a connection.*

6 *Email software allows you to send and receive emails.*

7 *You should get some anti-virus software on your computer so that it is less likely to get damaged by a computer virus.*

8 *When you buy peripherals for your computer they normally come with their own software, which you have to install.*

9 *Free software is available on the Internet and some of it is very good. Microsoft Office is not free and you should not use illegal copies of these.*

10 *All software is supplied with a licence that proves that you have paid for a legitimate copy.*

4

Getting started – first basics

In this chapter you will learn
- *how to switch your computer on and off*
- *how to use the mouse and keyboard*
- *about the Windows desktop*
- *how to open and close programs*
- *how to open and close folders*

4.1 Switching the computer on and off

To switch your computer on, you need to find the button that has this symbol on it.

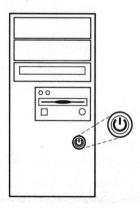

This is the on/off button although you should normally only use it to switch the computer on.

Press the on/off button and release – and wait.

The computer will now go through a start-up routine that may take a few minutes. If nothing appears on the screen, it may be that the monitor is not switched on. The monitor also has an on/off switch, so make sure that this is on. You can tell that the computer and monitor are on as there is a small (usually green) light that will light up when they are on.

Hints and tips

The start-up routine is carried out by the Windows operating system that we talked about in Chapter 1. It has to go through this routine every time you switch on. Windows will also switch the computer off when you tell it to, which is why you never need to use the on/off button to switch your computer off.

If it is a brand new computer, you will probably be prompted to set up a name and password for it. If this is the case, give it a sensible name (your own name for example) and a password that you will remember. It might be worth writing this down somewhere safe. When it has finished its routine, you will see the Windows desktop.

There may be other windows open on your desktop. This depends on how the computer has been set up. If you do have extra options other than those shown

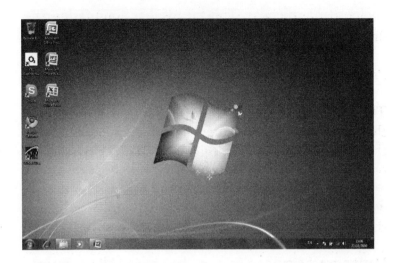

in our example, don't worry. You can ignore them for now and you will soon discover how to close any windows that you don't want.

Think of the desktop like a normal desktop – a flat surface with lots of things on it. You will always start at the desktop and will use it a lot, so you need to get used to it. The small pictures you can see are called icons. By double clicking on these with the mouse, you can open up programs and folders.

Also, note the Windows icon in the very bottom left-hand corner. This is referred to as the Start button and it opens a menu which will provide access to everything on your computer.

The Windows desktop can be customized. You can move the icons around and add your own background, called 'wallpaper'. You can also add 'gadgets' such as a clock or a calendar. This means that your desktop might not look exactly the same as the one shown here.

4.2 Using the mouse

To make things happen, you can either use the mouse or the keyboard. Your mouse will have at least two buttons called the left and right buttons. It may also have a scroll wheel between the two buttons.

As you move the mouse around on your mouse mat, it will move a small pointer on the screen. All programs work with a mouse – you simply point and then click on the icons and menus that you want to use.

Throughout this book, when you need to click on something on the screen, it will be shown in the text in single speech marks. For example, if you need to click on a menu on the screen called Save, the instruction will read either: Click 'Save' or Select 'Save'.

To use the mouse:

1 *Hold it lightly using the thumb on one side and your third and little fingers on the other. This leaves your first and second fingers free for clicking and using the scroll wheel. You might want to practise moving the mouse around and watching as the pointer moves.*
2 *As well as pushing the mouse around, you will also need to lift it slightly from time to time. The mouse only works if it is flat on your mouse mat, but*

sometimes you simply run out of mouse mat! When this happens, you need to lift the mouse off the mat and reposition it in the centre of the mouse mat before you start moving it again. This might be a bit tricky when you first start, so have a play until you feel more comfortable with it.

Hints and tips

Some mice are more sensitive than others, which means that the pointer will move by different amounts. If you use more than one computer, it might take a while to get used to a different mouse.

You can actually move the pointer all the way across the screen without having to move the mouse much at all using the lifting technique described here.

4.3 Clicking on things

There are three types of click:

▶ *A left click (known as a click). This is used mainly when you want to select something from a list or menu.*
▶ *A double left click (known as a double click). This is another thing that you might need to practise when you start. A double click is when you click twice on the left button, quite quickly. You use this when you click on icons.*
▶ *A right click. This provides access to hidden menus. Right clicks work only in certain places, as you will start to discover later.*

Let's practise the clicks now.

1 *First, from the desktop, click (that's a single left click) on the Windows icon in the very bottom left-hand corner.*

2 *Click on 'Documents'. This will then show a window that looks a bit like the one below. It is called a window because it opens in a frame. Don't worry if yours does not have exactly the same number of little yellow folders and icons in as this, but it should look something like this:*

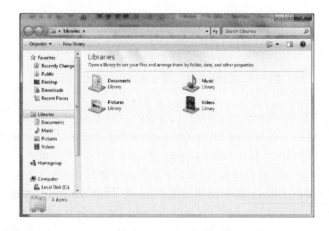

You will notice that there are three small icons in the top right-hand corner of the window. These are displayed in every window in every program.

The first one is called Minimize. This closes the window but leaves it available so that you can get it back later.

3 *Click on the 'Minimize' icon. The window closes, but if you look at the bar across the bottom of the screen (called the Taskbar), it is still available here. Any windows that you minimize will have a small icon in the Taskbar which you can click on to get it back to full screen. This feature is useful as it means you can have lots of different things open at the same time, and you can use the Taskbar to get to them quickly. If you hold your mouse over each icon, it will show a thumbnail view of that window to remind you what it is.*

4 *To re-open the 'Documents' window, click on the Windows Explorer icon now from the Taskbar at the bottom of the screen.*

The second icon is called Restore. This changes the size of a window from full screen (where it fills the screen) to a smaller size. The advantage of this is that you can have several smaller windows all open at the same time.

5 *Click on the 'Restore' icon now to see what happens.*

6 *Click on it again to restore it to its original size.*

The final icon is the cross. This closes the window. You will use this a lot as this is the main way of closing things down when you have finished with them.

To close this window:

7 *Click on the little cross in the very top right-hand corner of the window as shown.*

You have used a double click and a click to open and close a window. You are now back at the desktop.

8 *Move the mouse pointer somewhere on the desktop where there are no icons.*

9 *Right click. A hidden menu is displayed. This menu will be different depending on where you press the right click.*

10 *Click somewhere else on the desktop and the hidden menu will disappear again.*

Hints and tips

The scroll wheel comes in handy when you are looking at things on the screen that take up more than a screenful. If this is the case you have to scroll, or move up and down, and you can use the scroll wheel for this. We will use this for the first time in Chapter 6.

4.4 Using the keyboard

This is a bit more straightforward as it works in the same way as a typewriter. That is, you press the keys and whatever you type will appear on the screen.

When you are on the desktop you don't really need to type anything, but you will use it a lot in other programs. There are a few keys that carry out specific functions. You will be introduced to these as you need them, but it is worth pointing a few out now.

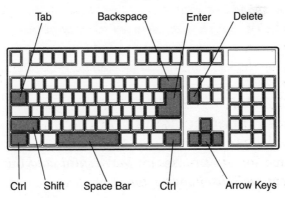

Throughout this book, when you need to press one of the keys its name will be shown in capitals. For example, if you need to press the ENTER key, the instructions will read: Press ENTER.

- ENTER: *You will use this key a lot. It is used to tell the computer you want to do something and is used when typing to start new lines.*
- SPACE: *The space bar is used to add spaces in between words when typing.*
- TAB: *This is really useful when you are filling in forms when you are on the Internet. It will move you from one part of the form to the next and saves you having to click.*
- SHIFT: *Allows you to type capitals and gives you access to all of the characters displayed at the top of the keys, for example, above the numbers.*
- CTRL: *Can be used for shortcuts. These are ways of doing things quicker. You will be told about these as you work through the book.*
- BACKSPACE and DELETE: *Used a lot when typing. They delete (erase) any characters that you have typed incorrectly.*
- ARROW KEYS: *Can be used like the mouse to move the pointer on the screen around (in some programs).*

4.5 Opening and closing programs

Programs are all of those things that you use your computer for, for example, word processing, or surfing the Internet. To do these things, you have to open the appropriate program. You open programs from the desktop in one of two ways:

- *Double click on the icon that represents the program on the desktop.*

- ▶ *Click on 'Start' (the windows icon in the very bottom left-hand corner)*
- ▶ *Click on 'All programs', find the program on the list and click on it.*

Hints and tips

All programs have little pictures associated with them. These are called icons. For example, Microsoft Word has a blue W and Internet Explorer has a blue E. There is also a label with the icon that tells you what program it is.

It is easiest to open programs from an icon, but sometimes the icon does not exist, so you have to go through the Start menu. To practise, we are going to open Microsoft Word. To open from an icon:

1 *Double click on the 'Word' icon.*  *The Word program will open and will look like this:*

2 *To close the program, click on the small cross in the top right-hand corner of the window.*

To open from the Start menu:

1 *Click on the Start button.*
2 *Move the mouse pointer to 'All Programs'. A list will now be displayed.*
3 *Find 'Microsoft Word' in the list and click on it. You may have to click on the option for Microsoft Office in the list first if you can't find it. The program will load.*
4 *Click on the cross to close the program.*

The process of opening and closing any program is exactly the same. This means there will always be either an icon, or if there is no icon, the name of the program will appear on the list in the Start menu. All programs can be closed by clicking on the cross in the top right-hand corner.

4.6 Opening and closing folders

Folders are where you save your work. When you first start off there are four libraries containing folders. These libraries are called Documents, Music, Pictures and Video and are organized like this to make it easier to find what you are looking for. Think of folders like normal paper folders. They are just somewhere to put your work. All work (whatever it is) is stored in files. We will start in a folder called Documents which at first will have nothing in it.

Hints and tips

It might help to think of your computer as an electronic filing cabinet. The folders are where you will store all of your work.

Folders have their own icon, which is a little yellow folder! Whenever you see a little yellow folder, it means that there is some work stored in it. Later on, you will make your own folders.

As a practice:

1 *From the desktop, double click on the 'Start' icon and click on 'Documents'. As an alternative you can click on the small yellow folder in the Taskbar at the bottom of the screen. This will take you to the last folder you had open or will show you the four libraries mentioned above.*
2 *This will open a new window that will show you all of the work that is stored in this folder. If it's a brand new computer, there will be nothing in it.*
3 *Click on the 'Start' icon in the bottom left-hand corner and open Word again.*

You have now got two things open: Documents and Word. You are now multi-tasking! To switch between the two things that are open, you just click on them in the Taskbar at the bottom of the screen as described previously. Try this now.

There is another way of switching between windows in Windows 7 called Aero Flip 3D. This lets you see 3D images of all of the windows that you have open. You can then scroll through them and select the one you want to work on. To do this:

1 *Hold down CTRL and the Windows logo key. Now press the TAB key. The screen will now look something like this:*

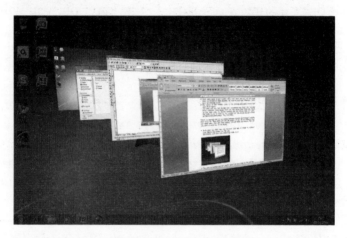

2 *You can now either use the scroll wheel on your mouse or the TAB key on your keyboard to scroll through all of the open windows. When you get to the one you want to work with, click the mouse on it or press ENTER. This window will then be shown full screen.*
3 *Click on 'Documents' in the Taskbar and then click on the cross in the top right-hand corner of the window to close it.*

Word will still be open. Leave it open for now, as we will use it to look at some of the standard features of software.

If you ever want to get back to your desktop quickly you do not have to close or minimize all the open windows.

1 *Move the mouse into the very right-hand bottom of the screen where you can see a small rectangle:*

2 *Hold the mouse over the rectangle and it will make any windows that are open transparent so you can see the desktop beneath.*
3 *Click on the rectangle and you are taken directly to the desktop.*
4 *Click on the rectangle again to go back to the last window that you were working on.*

4.7 Tabs

This book will introduce you to lots of different software. Although each program is used for different things, there are some standard features. This is quite useful because it means once you have learned how to do something in one program, you can transfer that skill to any program. You have already seen one standard feature in that all software opens in a window, and you need to click on the cross to close it.

One standard feature in Microsoft Office is the use of *tabs*. Tabs contain sets of options that you can choose from. The options are all of the different things that the software can do. Confusingly, the word tab here is absolutely nothing to do with the Tab key that you used in the previous section!

As you work through the book, you will be taken through many tab options. Some of the common ones are listed here. Tabs are usually shown at the top of the window after you have opened the program. In this example, the tabs for Word are shown, e.g. Home, Insert, Page Layout, etc. These menus will vary a bit depending on what program you are using but many of them are the same in all programs.

▶ *As you click on each tab it will reveal a different set of options. The options are grouped together. For example: the Home tab contains options for formatting the document; the Insert tab contains options for things you might want to insert like pictures or shapes. This can be quite confusing at first but as you start to use the programs more you will start to remember where everything is.*

In the very top left-hand corner you will see a very important icon called the Microsoft Office button.

This contains some of the most common actions that you are likely to need including opening, saving and printing documents. More on this later.

4.8 Switching off the computer

You might not want to do this just yet, but it is worth having a practice now. Remember that you don't actually press the on/off button to switch the computer off. Instead you do the following:

1 *Click on the 'Start' icon in the bottom left-hand corner.*
2 *Click on 'Shut Down' again from the options listed.*
3 *Click 'OK'.*

Your computer may take a while to switch itself off, but after a few seconds it will shut itself down. Note that you can access other options for shutting down by clicking on the small arrow to the right of the 'Shut down' option. For example, you can put your computer into 'Sleep' mode if you are planning to use it again soon. This reduces the time it takes to get up and running when you switch it back on again.

Hints and tips

It is important that you shut down the computer using this method. It carries out various checks as it shuts down to make sure that it is done properly. Switching off using the on/off key will cause problems when you come to switch on again. You should only use the on/off switch when the normal shut down routine won't work – this sometimes happens.

When the computer shuts down it should also turn off the monitor, so you probably do not need to switch this off separately.

IMPORTANT THINGS TO REMEMBER FROM THIS CHAPTER

1 *When you switch the computer on it will go through a routine that may take a few minutes. This is setting up the computer so that it works properly.*

2 *You use the mouse to move a pointer on the screen and then click on images to make things happen.*

3 *Your mouse has a left and right button. Different things happen depending on where you click and which button you use.*

4 *Your mouse may also have a scroll wheel that allows you to move the pointer up and down on the screen.*

5 *On your computer keyboard, in addition to the letters of the alphabet there are other keys, such as ENTER which have special functions.*

6 *You can open programs by clicking on small images called icons. Each program has its own icon so you can tell which is which.*

7 *Folders are locations on the computer where information is stored. For example, there is a folder for documents.*

8 *All programs and folders open in windows. You can have lots of open at the same time and flip between them in a number of ways.*

9 *You can close any window at any time by clicking on the little cross in the top right hand corner.*

10 *You need to switch off the computer via the Start menu so that it can close down properly. You should never switch it off using the on/off switch!*

5

Getting equipment and programs onto your computer

In this chapter you will learn
- *how to attach equipment to your computer*
- *how to put new programs on to your computer from CD or DVD*
- *how to access information stored on a CD or DVD*
- *about downloading software from the Internet*

5.1 Installing new equipment

The process of attaching new equipment is often called installing. You can also install or load new software. This is just computer-speak for adding something.

There are many occasions when you need to add a new piece of equipment to your computer. For example, you might want to:

- ▸ *attach a new printer*
- ▸ *attach a scanner*

- *plug in your digital camera*
- *add a web cam*
- *plug in some speakers*
- *add a new modem so you can get onto the Internet.*

Hints and tips

It is preferable to get your computer set up how you want it when you first buy it. Ask the shop to install the hardware and software for you so that it is ready to use when to get it. Most shops will do this without charging any extra.

The technical term for all of this equipment is hardware, and the process of attaching it to your computer and getting your computer to recognize it is pretty much the same regardless of what hardware you are adding.

When you buy new hardware, it will usually come with a set of instructions and a CD or DVD that contains the software or program needed to make it work. The CD or DVD will include an installation routine. This is a series of screens that you will be taken through.

The example shown here is for installing a new web cam and although all installation routines will vary slightly depending on what you are installing, you will find that most installation routines are similar to this one.

Sometimes, hardware will work on its own without having to go through an installation routine. You will find out as soon as you plug the device in. You will see a message at the bottom of the screen that reads 'New hardware found'. For example, if you plug in a memory stick it should just work automatically. With other devices, Windows will try and set it up for you via the Internet without having to use a CD or DVD.

If your new device does not work you will get a message on screen and you will then have to install the programs needed to make it work yourself off the CD or DVD. To do this:

1 *Open the CD/DVD drive on your computer by pressing the button next to it on your computer.*

2 *Put the CD/DVD that came with your hardware into the drive with the label facing up.*

3 *Close the CD/DVD drive by pressing the button again.*

4 *Wait for a few seconds and the CD/DVD will start to play automatically. If it plays automatically, go to step 8; if not, go to step 5.*

5 *If it does not start playing after a few seconds, click on the 'Start' icon in the bottom left-hand corner, click on 'Computer', then double click the CD or DVD drive as shown overleaf.*

6 *The CD/DVD will then open and the contents of the disk will be displayed in a new window. Double click the file named 'Set up' or 'Install'. Windows may show a message asking whether you want to confirm that you want to continue. This is here as a security measure and you will need to confirm that it is OK to continue.*

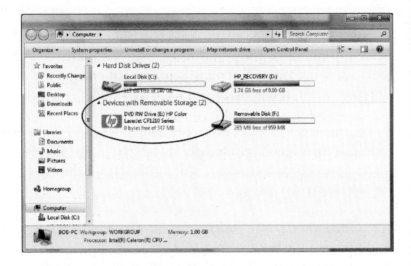

7 *The installation routine will now open and the first screen will be shown. In this case, it looks like this:*

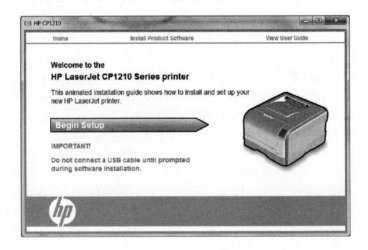

Hints and tips

Most installation routines have a main menu with a number of options on it. Select the one that installs the hardware. This will normally be the first one on the list and will be clearly labelled with the word 'Install', 'Add' or 'Set up'.

The next few screens will vary depending on what you are installing. This process of being led through several screens is called a wizard. Wizards may sometime ask some technical questions, but there is a simple rule: click 'Next'. The wizard will set up the new hardware using standard settings. Clicking the Next button accepts all of these settings.

8 *Click on 'Next' until there are no more screens and then click 'Finish'. Your new hardware is now installed. You may be prompted to switch the computer off and back on again for the new setting to work. You must do this if it tells you to.*

9 *You can now plug in the new hardware. This will normally be into the USB port. Make sure you plug it in with the little USB symbol facing up. It will only fit in the right way so don't force it.*

After a few seconds, you will see a message on your desktop telling you that new hardware has been found. It is now ready to use.

5.2 Installing new software

There are many occasions when you might need to do
this. For example:

- ▶ *You buy a new piece of hardware that comes with
  its own program, for example digital cameras
  are normally supplied with photograph editing
  software.*
- ▶ *You buy a new program that was not already on
  your computer.*
- ▶ *You get a free CD from a computer magazine that
  contains free software.*

The process is almost exactly the same as installing new
hardware. You will be presented with an installation
routine and you will need to follow the wizard to get
the new software installed properly.

When you buy software it will be supplied on a CD
or DVD. You can also download software directly
from the Internet. This example shows how to install
the software off a CD for an iPod™, which is called
iTunes™. Most software uses the same wizard as this.

Hints and tips

An iPod is a device that allows you to store
thousands of music tracks and listen to them via
earphones. They have become popular among all
age groups over the last few years. See Chapter 14
for more information.

1 *Open the CD/DVD drive on your computer.*

2 *Put the CD/DVD that came with your hardware into the drive with the label facing up.*

3 *Close the CD/DVD drive.*

4 *Wait for a few seconds and the CD/DVD will start to play automatically. If it plays automatically, go to step 8; if not, go to step 5. You may get a message asking you to confirm that you want to carry on.*

5 *If the CD/DVD does not start playing after a few seconds, click on the 'Start' icon in the bottom left-hand corner, click on 'Computer', double click the CD/DVD drive as described in section 5.1.*

6 *The CD/DVD will then open and the contents of the disk will be displayed in a new window.*

7 *Double click the file named 'Set up'. It may be called 'Install'.*

8 *The installation routine will now start and a screen will be shown that then disappears. Note that you might get a Windows message on the screen asking you to confirm that you want to install. You can click 'Yes' or 'OK' in these to continue.*

Hints and tips

When things are installing to your computer you will often be shown a status or progress bar. This is a visual representation of how long it will take to do its thing. You will see how quickly things are progressing as the bar moves, which is quite useful so you know whether to sit and wait, or go for a cup of tea.

Status: Copying new files

9 *The main menu will then be displayed. In this case it looks like this:*

10 *Like all wizards, you are prompted to read and then tick a box to agree to the licence agreements. You then click the 'Next' button to continue to the next screen. Each screen will present you with a range of options, which you change to suit your system. The general rule is to just keep clicking 'Next' until there are no more Nexts left to click, and then you click 'Finish'.*

11 *Click 'Next' until there are no more, and then click 'Finish'. You will then be shown a screen that tells you that you have successfully installed your new software. It may ask you to restart your computer to complete the installation process.*

12 *If you are told to restart your computer, you need to switch it off from the Start icon and then*

switch it back on again using the on/off button.
An alternative is to select Restart from the
shut down options.

When you have finished installing you can use the
software in one of two ways:

▸ *Click on the 'Start' icon in the bottom left-hand*
  corner.
▸ *Click 'All Programs'.*
▸ *Click on the new program from the list.*

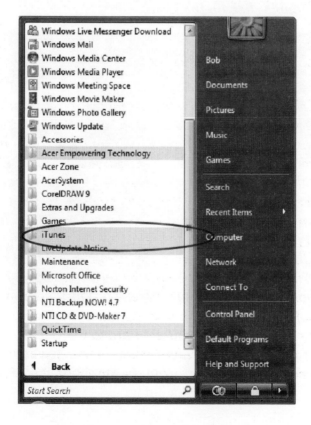

If there are lots of programs installed, it might take you a while to find it in the list, as illustrated here. It is the iTunes™ software that we have just installed.

Some installation routines will create a shortcut from the desktop. This means that it will put a little icon on the desktop (see next page) for you so that you can open it from here. If this is the case:

1 *Go to the desktop.*
2 *Find the icon for the new software.*
3 *Double click on the icon.*

This screenshot shows the shortcut to the iTunes software. It does not matter whether you open the software using the Start menu or the shortcut – they both take you to the same thing.

5.3 Accessing information from a CD or DVD

So far, you have used a CD or DVD to copy information
from the CD or DVD onto your computer. Once you
have done this, it means that you do not need to put the
CD or DVD in again, as the information that was on
the CD/DVD is now on your computer.

There are times where you want to get information
from a CD or DVD without actually installing it onto
your computer. For example, if you want to watch a
movie, or listen to a CD, or access something like an
encyclopaedia on CD, you do not have to install as
such, you just have to play the CD/DVD.

This process is similar to the one described in section 5.2
in that you insert the CD or DVD into the drive.

1 *Insert the CD/DVD that you want to play.*
2 *The CD/DVD may now autorun. This means that it
  will start to play automatically.*

If not:

3 *Click on the 'Start' icon.*
4 *Click on 'Computer'.*
5 *Select the CD or DVD drive.*
6 *On the CD/DVD cover it will tell you what to click on to make the CD/DVD play.*

The CD or DVD will now play. If it is something like an online encyclopaedia, it will have its own set of menus and you will need to follow the instructions on screen. If it is a music CD or a film DVD, it will start to play automatically using whatever media player software you have on your computer.

Hints and tips
There is more information on accessing music and film in Chapter 14.

5.4 Downloading software from the Internet

It is also possible to download (copy) software from the Internet. This means that rather than getting the software on CD, it can be transferred from the Internet onto your computer. This is not covered in detail in this chapter, as you need to be familiar with the Internet first. Chapters 10 to 16 cover use of the Internet in much more detail including downloading software.

IMPORTANT THINGS TO REMEMBER FROM THIS CHAPTER

1 *You will sometimes need to install new programs onto your computer. This might be ones you have bought or downloaded, or software that is supplied with a new peripheral.*

2 *The process of installing new software is similar regardless of what it is. After you have done this once it will be easier the next time.*

3 *Most installation routines lead you through the process step by step asking you to confirm at each stage.*

4 *You will be given an idea of how long installation will take as a progress bar will be shown. Larger programs can take several minutes.*

5 *When you install a new program, it will automatically appear in the list of programs under the Start menu.*

6 *Many installation routines also add a shortcut on your desktop. This is a small icon which you can click on to load the new program.*

7 *New software can be installed from a CD/DVD or downloaded (copied) from the Internet onto your computer.*

8 *Some software can be used direct from a CD/DVD without having to install it on your computer.*

9 *You should keep the original CD/DVD in case you ever need to install the program again.*

10 *Keeping the original CD/DVD is also proof of purchase.*

6

Writing letters using
Microsoft Word

In this chapter you will learn
- *how to type a letter*
- *how to save the letter*
- *how to change the size and style of the font*
- *how to format the letter*
- *how to correct mistakes*
- *how to correct spellings automatically*
- *how to print*

6.1 Getting started in Microsoft Word

Microsoft Word is a word processing program. It is designed to create all kinds of documents where the main thing that is required is lots of text. This chapter focuses specifically on writing letters and Chapter 7 looks at other types of documents that you might want to create. This is a good place to start as many of the basic computing skills are learned using Word.

1 *First, you need to open Word. To do this you can:*
  ▷ *Find the shortcut for it on your desktop and double click on it.*

  ▷ *Or click on the 'Start' icon in the bottom left-hand corner, click on 'All Programs', find 'Microsoft Word' and click on it.*

2 *Word will now open and you will be faced with a screen that looks like this.*

There are many other things on the screen and it is worth taking some time to understand what they all are.

The large white space is the page. Think of this as a piece of A4 paper onto which you are going to type your letter.

At the top of the screen:

MICROSOFT OFFICE BUTTON *contains commonly used options such as save and print.*

TABS *contain all of the options for actions you can perform in the software.*

TITLE BAR *shows the name of the document and the program being used.*

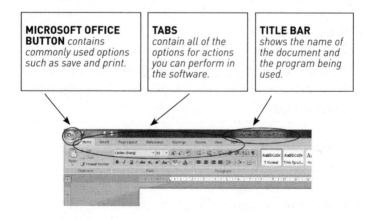

This is part of Windows and is always shown, whichever program you are in. It shows all of the programs and documents that are open. You can access the Start menu at any time by clicking on the Start icon 🌐 You can also access Windows Explorer 🪟 (to the right of the Start button) or re-open any programs that have been minimized. On the far right-hand side of the Taskbar you can see the time, date and some small icons. These icons are shortcuts to other programs and we look at them later.

Also note the small slider on the right-hand side at the bottom of the Word window. This is really useful as it allows you to zoom in and out of your document. Click and hold to move the slider and you can see the effect it has on the document. This just adjusts the zoom for viewing the document and has no effect on the actual size of the text when you come to print it out.

6.2 Scrolling up and down

On the far right-hand side of the screen is the scroll bar.

This allows you to move up and down the page, which is called scrolling. The lightest grey bar at the top indicates how much of the page you can see on the screen – about half in this case. To move to the bottom half of the screen:

1 *Click anywhere in the light grey section of the scroll bar and hold the left mouse button down.*
2 *While holding the button, move the mouse down.*
3 *This will move the page down so you can see the bottom half.*

To move the bar back up hold the left button down and move the mouse up.

Hints and tips

You can use the scroll wheel on your mouse here to scroll up and down.

6.3 Typing a letter

To get back to our letter, the first thing that needs typing is the address. You can use your own address here rather than our made-up one!

1 *In the top left-hand corner of the white space you will see a small line flashing – this is called the cursor. When you start typing, this is where the text will appear.*
2 *Type in the first line of the address as shown. For capital letters hold the SHIFT key* ⬚ *as you type the letter. Leave a single space between each word by pressing the SPACE BAR (the wide one at the bottom of the keyboard) once.*
3 *Press the ENTER key.* ⬚ *This moves the cursor down to the beginning of the next line.*

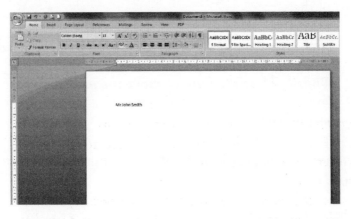

4 *Type the second line of the address and press ENTER.*
5 *Continue like this until every line of the address has been typed.*

At the moment the text is left-aligned. This means that it will all line up down an imaginary line on the left-hand side of the page.

Hints and tips

You will notice that there is a white space at the top and bottom of the page and down the sides that you cannot type into. These form the margins when you print out.

When you have finished typing, your document should look like this:

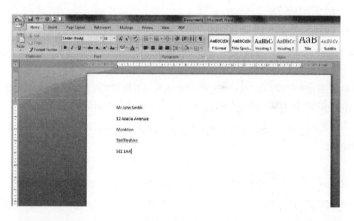

If you have made a mistake, you can correct it at any time. For example, let's pretend that the address was actually 14 Acacia Avenue.

1 *Use the mouse to point the cursor just before the 2 (in-between the 1 and 2). If you are not used to using a mouse, you may find it easier to position the cursor with the arrow keys.*

Mr John Smith

1⅟2 Acacia Avenue

Monkton

Steffieshire

SE1 1AA

2 *When you have got the mouse pointer between the*
1 and the 2, you need to click once. This puts the
cursor between the 1 and the 2.

3 *Press the DELETE key once. This will delete the*
letter or number that is to the right of the cursor –
the 2 in this case. 🔲

4 *Now type in a 4 so that the new address reads 14*
Acacia Avenue.

You might want to experiment with moving the cursor
and deleting and adding text. You can also use the
BACKSPACE key to delete text. This deletes letters to
the left of the cursor. 🔲

We now have the address, but it is on the wrong side of
the page. It needs to be right-aligned, which means that
it will line up to an imaginary line on the right-hand
side of the page. This involves highlighting (or selecting)
all of the text – this involves a new skill with the mouse.

1 *Point the mouse so that the cursor is just to the*
bottom-right of the address.

2 *Now click and hold down the left button.*

3 *Still holding on to the left button, move the mouse*
up to the top left-hand side of the address. You will

notice that the text becomes highlighted as shown in the diagram. This is sometimes called dragging.

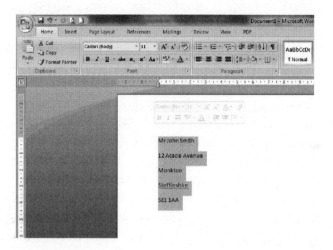

Hints and tips

Highlighting text like this is really useful because it means that you can work with whole blocks of text rather than just a letter or a number at a time. However, it is also a tricky manoeuvre with the mouse and might take a bit of practice.

4 *Once you have highlighted the text, you can let go of the left mouse button.*

5 *To move the highlighted text to the right, click on the 'right-align' button on the Home Tab at the top of the screen:*

6 *The block of text will move to the right. The rest of the letter needs to be left-aligned. Click to the right-hand side of the last line of the address (after the postcode).*

7 *Press the ENTER key once.*

8 *Click the 'left-align' button on the Home tab.*

The cursor moves back to the left and you can continue to type your letter. This means typing in the address of the person you are sending the letter to, the date, the salutation, the main body of the letter and the sign-off. The image on next page shows a standard letter. Notice how a line has been left between different parts of the letter. You can do this by pressing ENTER twice at the end of the line.

Hints and tips

When you get to the end of the line, you do not need to press ENTER to start a new line. Word will wrap the text for you. This means that when it runs out of space on the line, it will automatically start typing on the line below. The only time you need to press ENTER is when you want to start a new paragraph or leave a line.

_____

6.4 Saving the letter

When you are working on your computer you need to save your work on a regular basis. This is very important. If you do not save your work regularly you could lose everything you have done, which is frustrating. This applies to everything that you do, not just Word.

There is a folder already set up on your computer called Documents. For now, you should save everything you do into this folder.

Hints and tips

It is possible to lose your work accidentally perhaps by closing a program, or by deleting the wrong thing. You should save your work every 10 minutes to be on the safe side.

To do this:

1 *Click on the Microsoft Office button in the top left-hand corner.*

2 *The following screen will be displayed, click on 'Save' as shown:*

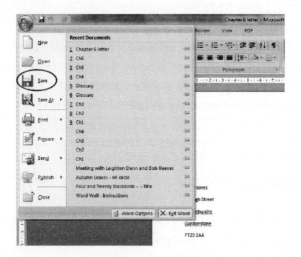

3 *Everything that is saved goes into what is called a file. You must give every file a name so that you know what is in it. In the box where it says 'File Name' you can now give a name to the document. Type in 'Chapter 6 letter' as shown and press ENTER.*

Hints and tips

Try to give your files sensible names. You might want to come back to this letter in a few weeks' time, so you will need a name that explains what is in it. If you call your file Document1 then you will not remember what is in it.

The document is now saved permanently. You will be able to come back to this document at any time, as it

will just stay in this folder forever (or until you choose to delete it).

Next time you save the file, you will not be asked for the name again, it will just save the changes you have made using the same name. Every time you click on 'Save', it saves the latest version of the file.

As a slightly quicker alternative to saving, just to the right of the Microsoft office button is the **Quick Access Toolbar**. This contains a number of shortcuts to commonly used functions. One of these is the Save option highlighted above. If you click on this it works in exactly the same way as going via the Microsoft Office button.

6.5 Changing the font

The font is the style of text that appears on the screen. There are hundreds of different styles and sizes to choose from, and you can add other features to the font such as underline, bold and italic.

For example:

This font is called Times New Roman and it is in 'point size' 12.

This is what it looks like in **bold**, underlined and *italic*

This one is called Arial, also in size 12, and this is size 14 and this is 18.

Most of the time you need only one or two fonts and if you are typing letters, point size 11 or 12 is usually fine. The standard setting is Calibri, size 11 and that is what your letter is.

To change the font:

1 *Highlight the whole letter using the method that you used to highlight the address earlier.*

2 *Click on the little arrow to the right of where it currently says Calibri (Body).*

3 *Select 'Arial' from the list that is displayed. All of the text will now change to the Arial font.*

6.6 Checking the spelling

You may notice as you type that some of the words have red squiggly lines underneath them and some might have green squiggly lines under them. These are where you have used words that the computer's dictionary does not recognize:

▶ *The red lines indicate spellings that it does not recognize.*

▶ *The green lines indicate mistakes that it thinks you have made with your grammar (cheeky thing).*

Red lines do not mean that you have necessarily spelled the word wrong. It just means that the computer does not recognize it. This might be because the word is a name, or an English spelling of a word that it wants to spell in American! You can just ignore the red lines – they will not print. However, if the word is spelled wrong you can either:

1 *Move the cursor to the word, click, press the DELETE key to delete wrong letters or the whole word, and retype.*

Or

2 *Right click on the word and you will be given suggested spellings as shown in the diagram.*

3 *If the correct spelling is on the list you can click on it and the incorrect word will be replaced with the one you have chosen.*

4 *If the correct spelling is not shown, you will need to click back in the letter and retype the word as described in step 1.*

Hints and tips

You can add words to the computer's dictionary by clicking on 'Add' in the list. If you do this, the next time you use the word, it will be recognized.

6.7 Printing the document

You can print out any document. A printout is a paper copy of what you see on the screen. When you are typing in Word, the white space on the screen represents a piece of A4 paper. Therefore, what you see on the screen is what you will get when you print out. However, the dimensions of the screen are not big enough to view the whole page so you need to use Print Preview to be able to see the whole document.

The Print Preview option is accessible through the Microsoft Office button but because you will probably use it a lot, we will set up Word so that there is a shortcut to it in the Quick Access Toolbar.

1 *Click on the small arrow on the right-hand side of the Quick Access Toolbar and click on 'Print Preview':*

2 *This will put the Print Preview icon into the Quick Access Toolbar so it should now look like this:*

3 *Click on the 'Print Preview' icon. This will then display as screen that will show how the printout will look. If you are happy with this you can click on the 'Print' icon in the left-hand corner. If you want to make further changes you can click on the red cross labelled 'Close Print Preview' and go back and make further changes to your document.*

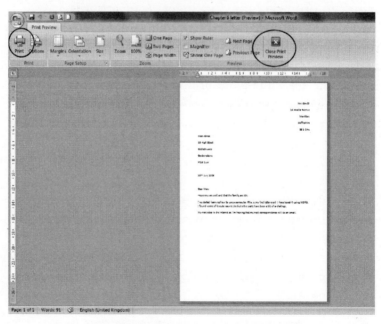

6.8 Closing the document

When you have finished with a document you need to close it.

1 *Make sure that you have saved the file as described earlier.*
2 *Click on the small cross in the top right-hand corner of the screen.*

This will close down the document and the Word program and take you back to the desktop.

IMPORTANT THINGS TO REMEMBER FROM THIS CHAPTER

1 *Microsoft Word is a word-processing program and can be used to create all kinds of text-based documents.*

2 *When you use Word most of the screen is taken up by white space. Think of this as a blank piece of paper onto which you type your document.*

3 *Word is a good place to start as there are many features that are common with other software.*

4 *Word is also a good place to practice your typing skills, which you will need whenever you are using the computer, particularly when sending emails.*

5 *One of the big advantages of using a computer is that it is easy to correct any mistakes before saving and printing the final version.*

6 *It is possible to work with blocks of text, for example, moving whole sentences and paragraphs around.*

7 *There are various ways in which you can format text by changing the style, size, colour and positioning.*

8 *You need to save your work with a suitable name into an appropriate library and folder. It is best to start with to save documents into the library called 'Documents'.*

9 *Anything you create is stored in a file. You give the file a file name so that you can remember what it is if you ever need to go back to it again.*

10 *You can print the document, previewing it first to check that it fits the page neatly.*

7

Writing minutes and other types of documents

In this chapter you will learn
- *how to create a heading for a document*
- *how to use bullet points and numbered points*
- *how to cut and paste text*
- *how to copy and paste text*
- *how to delete blocks of text*
- *how to undo and redo*
- *how to add an image to a document*
- *more about printing*

7.1 Adding a heading to a document

Most documents that you type need to have a heading to tell the reader what the document is. Microsoft Word can be used for typing any kind of document.

For example:

▶ *Minutes from a meeting (the example used in this chapter).*
▶ *Your great unfinished novel.*
▶ *An essay for a course you are taking.*
▶ *Lists of instructions or things to do.*

All of these will need headings and even subheadings. These need to stand out from the rest of the text and the way to do this is by changing the font (style of typing) and the alignment (where the text is positioned).

In this example, we will put the heading in bold and will centre it in the middle of the page.

1 *Open Word.*
2 *Type the following text 'Village Hall Meeting Minutes April 2010'.*

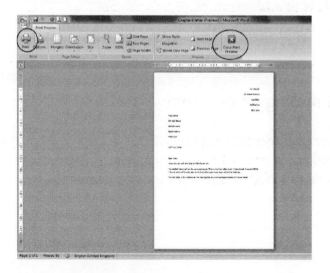

3 *Highlight the text. There are two ways of doing this here.*

> *You could hold the left mouse key and drag the mouse pointer across the text as described in the previous chapter.*

> *You can move the mouse to the left-hand side at the beginning of the line as shown in the diagram. Notice how the mouse pointer has changed to an arrow. Click once and the whole line will be highlighted.*

4 *Make the heading bold by clicking on the 'Bold' icon and increase the size of the font to 14 by clicking on the little arrow to the right of the 12, and then selecting 14 from the list:*

5 *Centre the title by clicking on the 'centre align' icon:*

6 *Press ENTER twice. This will move the cursor down two lines.*

7 *Click on the 'left-align' icon to move the cursor back to the left-hand side.*

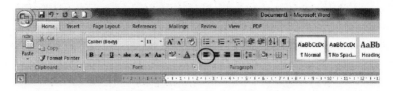

7.2 Using bullet points and numbered points

We can now continue with the rest of the document. Let's say there were five items on the agenda for the meeting:

1 *Type in the following five items, pressing ENTER after each one:*
   Apologies
   Village Hall bookings for July
   Fundraising events
   Progress of the roof repairs
   Any other business
2 *As this is a list, we can use either bullet points or numbered points to show this.*
   ▷ *This is a bullet point*
   2 *This is a numbered point*
3 *Highlight the list of five items by holding the left mouse button and dragging the mouse pointer over the text.*

4 *If you want bullet points, click the 'bullet point' icon. For a numbered list click the 'numbered points' icon.*

Bullet list   Numbered list

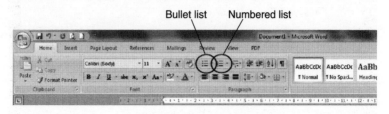

5 *Your list will be changed so that it has either bullets or numbers on it. Save your work at this point. Name the file: Village Hall Meeting Minutes April 2010.*

6 *Click underneath the list so that you can continue typing the minutes. We have made up some text as shown in the image on next page.*

7 *Highlight the subheadings and make them bold.*

Hints and tips

You can see that the use of **bold** is quite effective in making things stand out. You can also use *italics* and <u>underline</u>. However, you only really need to use one of these three methods to make things stand out.

Village Hall Meeting Minutes April 2010

1. Apologies
2. Village Hall bookings for July
3. Fundraising events
4. Progress of the roof repairs
5. Any other business

Apologies

Mr and Mrs Smith send their apologies. They are on holiday this week.

Village Hall bookings for July

The hall has been booked every Saturday night in July for wedding receptions.

Fundraising events

The summer fair will take place on June 20th.

Progress of roof repairs

We are a long way from having sufficient funds to pay for the roof repairs.

Any other business

There is an ongoing problem with lack of parking in front of the hall. We have also been receiving complaints about on-street parking from local residents.

7.3 Cutting and pasting text

One big advantage of computers is that anything you do can be edited. This means that things can be changed without having to start all over again. For example, if you wanted to move some text from one part of the document to another, you can do this without having to retype the text. This is called cut and paste. You cut the text from one place and paste it to another.

In this example, we will move the second sentence of the paragraph titled 'Progress of roof repairs' so that it is before the first sentence.

1 *Highlight the text that you want to move. In this case, it is the whole of the second sentence.*

Progress of roof repairs

We are a long way from having sufficient funds to pay for the roof repairs. The builders have been able to stop the leaks for now, but a more permanent repair is needed before next winter.

Any other business

2 *Right click on the highlighted text and then click on 'Cut' from the menu that is displayed.*

3 *Move the mouse and click so that the cursor is just to the left of the first sentence as shown:*

Fundraising events

The summer fair will take place on June 20th.

Progress of roof repairs

We are a long way from having sufficient funds to pay for the roof repairs.

Any other business

There is an ongoing problem with lack of parking in front of the hall. We have also been receiving complaints about on-street parking from local residents.

4 *Right click and then click on 'Paste' from the menu that is displayed. The highlighted text will now move before the first sentence.*

Hints and tips

You can use cut and paste to move any amount of text from one place to another. A variation is to copy and paste. To do this you choose 'Copy' instead of 'Cut'. This duplicates the highlighted text (makes a copy of it), rather than moving it.

7.4 Deleting blocks of text

A similar technique can be used to delete whole blocks of text. In the previous chapter you learned how to delete single letters at a time using the DELETE and BACKSPACE keys. However, you may wish to delete larger blocks of text.

To do this:

1 *Highlight the block of text that you want to delete. Use the same method as described previously.*
2 *Press the DELETE key. The text will now disappear.*

7.5 Undo and Repeat

It is quite common to make mistakes when using a computer. Sometimes you add something you didn't mean to and sometimes you delete something you didn't mean to (which is much worse).

There is a 'get out of jail card' and it's called Undo. This does exactly what it says – if you click on it, it undoes the last thing you did. If you click on it again, it undoes the thing before that – and so on. It is particularly useful if you have just deleted something by mistake.

To undo the deleting that we have just done:

▶ *Click on the 'Undo' button, which you will find on the Quick Access Toolbar in the top left-hand corner of the screen:*

This will undo the delete.

Hints and tips

You can use undo in all programs, not just Word. You can also use Repeat, which is the button to the right of Undo. This re-does whatever you did last.

7.6 Adding images to your document

There are different methods for adding in images to your documents. This chapter focuses on the use of ClipArt. There is more about working with images in Chapters 21 to 23 and 27.

ClipArt is available in all Microsoft software and is a library of images. Most of these are cartoon-style images, but some photographs are available too.

To insert an image from ClipArt:

1 *Click in your document, where you want your picture to be displayed.*
2 *Click the 'Insert' tab at the top of the screen.*
3 *Select 'ClipArt'.*
4 *The ClipArt window will now open on the right-hand side of the screen:*

5 *You can use the 'Search for' box at the top to type in what you are looking for. For example, type 'roof' into the search box and press ENTER or click on the 'Go' button. Make sure that the 'Search in' box reads 'All collections'. If it does not, click on the small arrow to the right of the box and click on 'All collections'.*

6 *There is also an option called 'Clipart on Office Online' in the bottom right hand corner. Clicking on this will link you to a website where many more ClipArt images are available. A list of images related to roofs is now shown. The images will vary from computer to computer depending on what version of ClipArt is installed. You may need to scroll down to see all of the images available.*

7 *When you have found the image you want, double click and it will appear on your document at the cursor location, as per point 1.*

The image will go in at a set size. You may want to reposition or resize the image. There is more information on this in Chapter 22.

7.7 Printing your document

In the previous chapter, you learned how to use Print Preview and how to click on the 'Print' icon to get a document to print. There are quite a few other printing options available. Two of the most useful are telling the printer to print in either colour or black and white, and printing several copies of the same document.

To access these options:

1 *Click on the Microsoft Office button and move the mouse onto the 'Print' option but do not click just yet. It will look like this:*

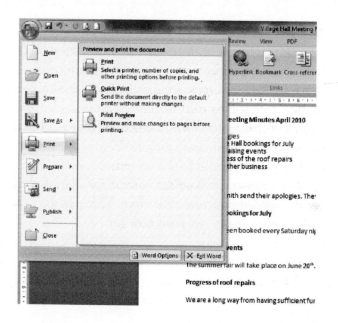

2 *Select 'Print', which is the first of the three options. This screen will now be displayed:*

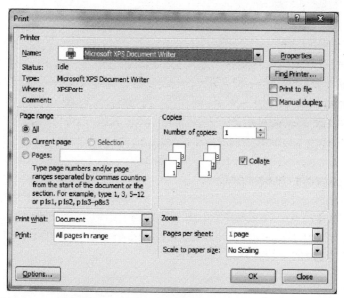

3 To *print several copies of the same document,
type the number that you want in the box labelled
'Number of copies'.*
4 *Click 'OK'.*

To select whether to print in colour or black and white:

1 *Click on 'Properties'.*
2 *Find the option and select 'Color' or 'Black and
White' as appropriate and click 'OK'. It may be
called 'grey scale' on your printer.*

IMPORTANT THINGS TO REMEMBER FROM THIS CHAPTER

1 *You can make your documents more attractive and easier to read with a few simple formatting options such as creating a heading in bold text.*

2 *Bullet points and numbered points are a good way of breaking up blocks of text to make your document more readable.*

3 *Cutting and pasting is when you move something, e.g. a block of text, from one part of the document to another.*

4 *It is possible to delete individual letters or to highlight and delete whole blocks of text.*

5 *If you go wrong, Undo will undo whatever you did last. It will remember all of your actions so you can use it to undo several steps.*

6 *Use the Repeat button if you accidently undo the wrong thing.*

7 *You can add images to your documents. These might be cartoon style images, photographs or shapes.*

8 *ClipArt is a library of images that can be added to your documents.*

9 *Any images you use can be positioned around the text to create a professional looking document.*

10 *There is a range of print options such as printing in black and white or colour, or printing several copies of the same document.*

8

....

Keeping in touch using email

In this chapter you will learn
- *what email is*
- *how to set up and use web-based email software*
- *how to read and reply to emails*
- *how to send emails*
- *how to add people to your email address book*

_____

8.1 Email software

There are two main types of email software. The first is software such as Live Mail or Outlook, which come as part of the Microsoft Office package. These are installed on your computer and you run them from your desktop in the same way as other programs.

The second type is what is called web-based email. With these, you do not need to have email software on your computer, as you can get access to it using the Internet. Web-based email is generally free. For example, Hotmail® is a free-to-use web-based email. You may also be given free email addresses from your Internet Service Provider (the company you get your Internet connection from). For example, BT, AOL and Tiscali all provide free web-based email.

It does not really matter which one you choose. You might find it easier to use one of the web-based ones first as you will not need to set up any software to get it to work.

This chapter will use Hotmail as an example and will show you how to set up and use an email account. All email software works slightly differently although they all have the same basic functions. Therefore, even if you do not use Hotmail, the basic principles described here will apply. If you already have an email address, then you can skip the section on setting up an email account.

8.2 Email basics

Email stands for electronic mail and the easiest way to think of it is as an electronic letter. You do not have to print it out and send it – instead, it is sent electronically over the Internet. Therefore, you must have Internet access in order to use email.

Like normal mail, emails are sent and received using addresses. All email addresses follow the same format. For example:

glynishubblethwaite@hotmail.co.uk

The bit before the @ sign is usually used to identify the individual, and the bit after is the name of the email provider.

Hints and tips

Email has been around for many years now and has millions of users. Therefore you might not get the email address you would like as there is probably already someone out there with the same name as you who has already bagged the address.

8.3 Setting up an email address in Hotmail

When you come to choose your email address, it can be anything you like, but you might find someone already has it and you have to think again. You should type the address in lower case letters with no spaces in between words e.g. snugglekiss@hotmail.co.uk rather than SnuggleKiss@hotmail.co.uk. Make sure that you select hotmail.co.uk as the last part of the address.

Bear in mind that you will be giving your address out so that people can email you. Therefore, snugglekiss@ hotmail.com might seem like a good idea now, but might be a bit embarrassing when you send an email to the vicar!

Skip this section if you already have an email address.

First you will need to log on (get on) to the Internet.

1 *Click on the 'Internet Explorer' icon in the bottom left-hand corner of the Taskbar.*

Hints and tips

When you start Internet Explorer, it will load your home page. The home page can be set to any page you like and to start with, will be set to whatever the shop set it to when you bought it. It might also be set to the home page of your Internet Service Provider (e.g. AOL, BT, Tiscali, etc.).

Web pages are constantly changing so the pictures of screens that you seen here might be different by now. If this is the case, the same or similar options will still be available to you. They might just be in a different place on the screen.

2 *In the address bar near the top of the screen (shown below), type 'www.hotmail.com' and press ENTER.*

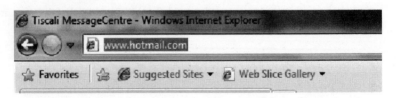

3 *After a few moments the Hotmail home page will be displayed. This is their main page. There are hundreds of other pages that lead off from this one. Click on the link to 'Sign Up' as shown below.*

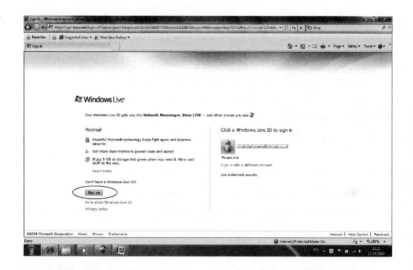

Hints and tips

Web pages like this one contain lots of links (also known as hyperlinks) to other pages, also known as hyperlinks. When you click on a hyperlink, the browser will take you to another web page.

4 *You will be signing up to something called 'Windows Live'. This will give you access to: Hotmail for free emailing: Messenger, which is an instant chat website (more on these in Chapter 13); and Xbox Live, which allows people to play Xbox games against each other over the Internet.*

5 *You are now asked to complete a form on the screen. This may take quite a while, especially if you have never filled in an online form before. You will find that as you use the Internet more, you will be asked to fill in lots of forms. This is because the websites want you to register your details with* *them before you can use their free services. There is guidance available at each stage.*

6 *You will be asked what email address you would like. It can be anything that is not already in use, but it must have hotmail.co.uk as the last part of the address.*

7 *You will also be asked for a password. Choose something that is easy to remember.*

8 *Complete the rest of the form and follow the instructions on the screen. If you go wrong or miss anything out, you will be asked to do those bits again.*

9 *When you have filled in the form, you need to click on the 'I accept' button at the bottom to accept the Hotmail terms and conditions. You might need to scroll down to get to the bottom of the page.*

10 *A screen will then be displayed informing you that your email address is ready to use.*

11 *The first time you use Hotmail it tries to subscribe you to lots of email services. You can have a read through to see if you want any of them, but you don't have to subscribe to any. To move on without subscribing, scroll all the way to the bottom and click 'Continue'.*

8.4 Reading an email

To read an email:

1 *Open your email software. In this case we are using Hotmail so start Internet Explorer either by clicking on 'Internet' in the 'Start' icon, or clicking on the*

Internet Explorer icon in the Taskbar in the bottom left-hand corner of the screen.

2 *Type 'www.hotmail.com' into the address bar as before. You will notice that Internet Explorer remembers what you have typed in before, so as you start to type the first few letters, it will automatically show you the full address. You can type in the full address or simply click on it when you see it displayed. The Hotmail home page will then load and will look something like this:*

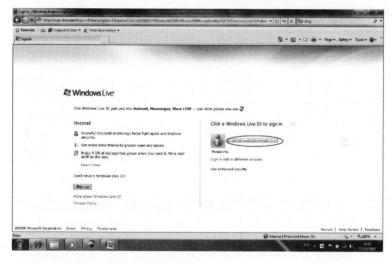

3 *Websites are quite clever and will remember you. You will probably find that the Hotmail website already knows that it is you and that your email address is already shown on the page. If so you will not need to 'log in' as shown here.*

4 *Your email address should already be shown. If not, type it in the box next to 'E-mail address', click on it and then type in your password when prompted. Then click 'Sign In'.*

5 *Find where it says 'Mail' and click on it. Your Inbox is where any email that has been sent to you will be kept. It will show you how many messages you have got, who they are from, how many of them you have already read and how many are new. The image below shows the Inbox of a Hotmail account. Yours may look slightly different but will have all of the same features. This shows ten unread message(s).*

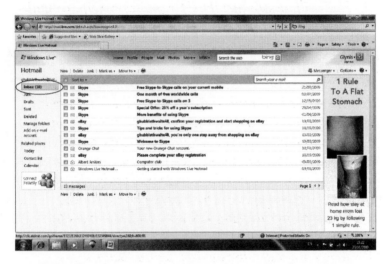

6 *To read a message, double click on it in the list (there are ten in this case) and the whole message will be displayed.*

7 *When you have read the message you can go back to the Inbox by clicking on the link to it as shown. You can then read your other messages. The Inbox is usually on the left-hand side of the screen.*

Hints and tips

The process of opening your email software might be slightly different if you are not using Hotmail.

8.5 Replying to an email

If you want to reply to an email:

1 *Open your email software and open the message as described above.*
2 *After you have read the message, click on 'Reply'.*
3 *This will automatically set your screen up to send an email back to this person. You do not have to type in their email address as this has been done for you.*
4 *The Hotmail screen looks like the one overleaf and yours will look similar. You can see there is a box with the address of the person to whom you are replying. The original message is still shown in the main box and you can type your message in above it. Type in your reply. The box that you are typing into works just like Word. You type in, pressing ENTER to leave lines for new paragraphs.*
5 *When you have finished, click on 'Send'.*

Your email is then sent to the other person's Inbox and they will receive it next time they check their emails.

Hints and tips

You may receive a lot of junk email. This is called spam and is usually from companies trying to sell you things. The best bet is to simply ignore this and delete it using the 'Delete' option. There is more information on Internet security in Chapter 16.

8.6 Sending an email

To send an email, you need to know the address of the person you are sending it to. Apart from that, it is similar to replying to an email as described in the previous section.

1 *Open your email software as described earlier.*
2 *Click on 'New'. In your email software this might be called 'New Message', 'Create Mail' or 'Compose'. You will be presented with a screen that allows you to address, type and send the email. In Hotmail it looks like this:*

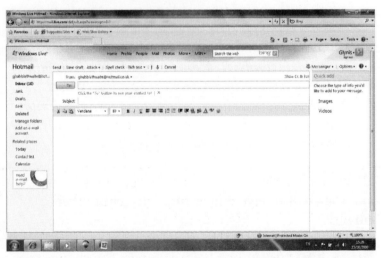

3 *In the 'To:' box, type the email address of the person you want to send the email to. Make sure you type the email address accurately or your email*

will not get through. To get the @ sign you will need to press the SHIFT key with the single speech mark (').

4 *The 'Cc:' box allows you to type in another address. If you want to send the same message to two people at the same time, you can put a second address in here. This can be left blank.*

5 *The 'Bcc:' box allows you to send a 'blind' copy to a third person. This means that they will get a copy of the message, but any other people to whom you sent or cc'd it will not know that they got a copy. This can be left blank.*

6 *The 'Subject:' box is so that the person receiving the message knows what it is about. They will see this before they read the full message so it worth putting something in here.*

7 *The main box is for the body of the message. You can type as much as you like in here. It works like Word – you just keep typing, pressing ENTER when you want to leave a line for a new paragraph.*

8 *When you have finished your message, click on 'Send'.*

Hints and tips

If you are typing a long email, you might want to use the 'Save Draft' option. This saves what you have typed so far so that you can get it back if something goes wrong before you get the chance to send it. There is a 'Drafts' folder underneath your Inbox where the drafts will be saved to.

8.7 Using the address book

You can put any addresses that you want to use into an address book. This is just like a normal address book. The advantage of using this is that you don't need to remember all those email addresses with the @ sign in them.

In Hotmail and some other email software, the address book is called 'Contacts'.

1 *In your email software, click on 'Contact list'. (It may be called 'Address Book' or 'Addresses'.)*
2 *Click 'New'. (It might be called 'New Contact'.)*
3 *You can now type in the email address and other details of your contacts. Type email addresses carefully.*
4 *Now when you want to send an email to anyone in your address book, rather than typing their name into the 'To' box, you just click on the word 'To' and your address book will be displayed. You can then select the name from the list.*

IMPORTANT THINGS TO REMEMBER FROM THIS CHAPTER

1 *There are two main types of email software. The first is installed on your computer. The other type is accessed over the Internet.*

2 *There are advantages and disadvantages to both but it is probably easier to start with one of the web-based email programs such as Hotmail.*

3 *Your ISP will probably supply you with a number of free email addresses (although many people only need one).*

4 *Emails and electronic messages are a bit like the modern equivalent of a letter, although often they are much less formal.*

5 *The first task is to set yourself up with an email address, which means registering with an email provider and filling in an online form.*

6 *The two most common functions of email are receiving them and sending them.*

7 *You can send emails either by replying to an email or by typing in the email address of the person you want to send a message to.*

8 *Everyone's email address is unique so it is important to get it correct. If you don't, someone else might receive the message.*

9 *All email software has an address book feature where you can store people's contact details. This saves typing in the address every time.*

10 *All emails arrive in your 'Inbox' and you can store messages for as long as you want them.*

9

Pictures and other attachments via email

In this chapter you will learn
- *how to open an email attachment*
- *how to save an email attachment on your computer*
- *how to send an email attachment*

9.1 Opening email attachments

When you receive an email message, if there is anything attached to it, you will see a paperclip icon next to the Subject.

Hints and tips
There are lots of different types of email, but they all use this symbol to show that there are attachments.

1 *Open your email software in the normal way. As in the previous chapter, we are using Hotmail. If you have other email software, all of the options will be* *virtually the same, but they might look different on the screen.*

2 *Look for the paper clip symbol. If there is one, it means that the email has an attachment. In the example on next page top, Albert has received an email with an attachment from his friend Glynis Hubblethwaite.*

3 *Open the email by clicking on it. The full message is then displayed and the attachments are listed as shown. In this example there are two files attached. One is called Flowers 1.jpg and the other is called Flowers 2.jpg. The jpg part tells you what kind of file it is. A jpg file is a photograph. You will start to recognize these three-letter codes as you use your computer more and more.*

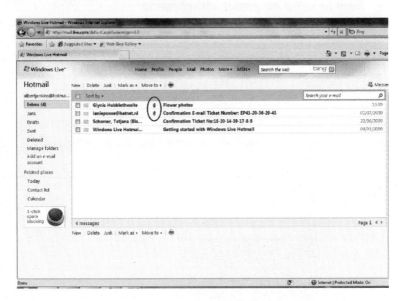

Hints and tips

Notice how the two files in this example have slightly different names. Your computer will not let you give two files exactly the same name.

4 *Some email software will show you the attachments underneath the text of the email as is the case here. If this is the case, you can scroll down to view the attachments. If not:*

5 *To open the attachment, click on it.*

6 *Depending on your software, different things might happen now. In Hotmail, and some other email, the software will scan the file to check for viruses. Viruses are programs created by people with nothing better to do. They attach themselves to emails and if they infect your computer they can cause it a lot of damage. You may get a message asking if it is OK to open the attachment. If you know who it is from you can click 'Open' to continue.*

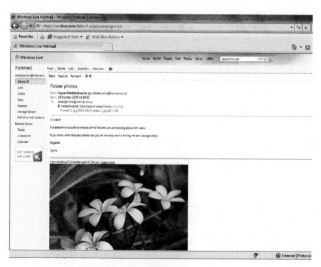

7 *If your software does not have a virus checker, the attachment will open. In this case, it will display the photograph of the flowers.*

Hints and tips

Make sure that you have anti-virus software on your computer. See Chapter 16 for more advice on this.

8 *Once you have viewed the picture, click on the cross in the top right-hand corner of the window that is displaying it.*
9 *Now click on 'Back' at the top of the screen to get back to the email message.*
10 *You can now view the other attachment in the same way.*

There may be many files attached to an email and you will need to go through each of them one by one to view them.

9.2 Saving email attachments

The email attachments are embedded in the email that they were sent with. If you delete the email, you will also delete the attachments. In this case, it would mean that we would no longer have these photographs.

If you want to keep a copy of the attachments, you need to save them onto your computer. You already have a folder called Pictures and this is as good a place as any to put them.

Hints and tips

You can make your own folders to save files into if you want to. This is covered in Chapter 19.

To save an attachment:

1 *When the picture is displayed, click on 'File' at the top of the window that is displaying the picture.*
2 *Click on 'Make a copy'. The following screen is then displayed*

3 *Pictures will automatically be saved into a folder called 'Pictures library'. It will be saved under your user name that you (or whoever set your computer up) set up when you first got the computer.*
4 *The computer will automatically use the same name to save the file. You can change it by typing a new*

file name or keep the suggested name and click on 'Save'.

5 *Repeat the same process for each attachment.*

The picture is now saved into your Pictures library. We will be looking at how to manage your files and folders in Chapter 19.

9.3 Sending an attachment

If you want to send an attachment, you first need to know the name of the file that you want to attach, and the name of the folder or library that it is in. In this example, we will show the process that Glynis went through when she attached the two pictures of the flowers and sent them to Albert. The two files that she sent were called Flowers 1.jpg and Flowers 2.jpg and were in her Pictures library.

1 *Open up your email software.*
2 *Type in the address, subject and message in the usual way. You are now ready to add your attachment.*
3 *Click on 'Attach'. The command might have a slightly different name in other email software. It might be called 'Insert' or 'Insert Attachments' or 'File Attachments' or just 'Attachments'.*
4 *Select 'File'.*
5 *Double click on 'Libraries' and then double click on 'Pictures'. Note that you can move to any of your*

libraries and attach any files at this point. Libraries might contain photographs, documents or other files. There is more about managing your libraries in Chapter 19.

6 *Double click on 'Flowers 1' (or whatever other file you wish to attach), wait for it to attach itself and then repeat the process on 'Flowers 2'. These files are now attached to the email.*

7 *Click 'Send' in the usual way. Your email and the attachments will now be sent to the email address that you typed in.*

Hints and tips

Different files are different sizes. Size refers to how much space they take up inside the computer. Photographs can get quite big. This means that they might take a while to attach themselves.

9.4 Attaching different types of file

We have attached photographs in this case, but you can attach any type of file in exactly the same way described above. We were using photos so the files were saved into the Pictures library that is already set up on your computer.

To send other file types you just need to know what they are called (the file name) and where they are (the folder name).

For example, you might want to send a copy of the Village Hall meeting minutes to someone. This is a Word file and is stored in the 'Documents library'.

1 *Follow exactly the same process as before, but rather than looking in 'Pictures library' when you see this screen, look in 'Documents library'.*
2 *Find the file called 'Village Hall Meeting Minutes' and double click on it. This file is now attached to the email.*

IMPORTANT THINGS TO REMEMBER FROM THIS CHAPTER

1 *An email attachment is a file that is sent along with an email.*

2 *The file could contain any type of information for example, a document or photograph.*

3 *A paper clip symbol is used to indicate that an email has an attachment with it.*

4 *You can open the attachment and view the content of the file.*

5 *You can save a copy of the attachment onto your own computer.*

6 *You can send attachments to other people using email.*

7 *You can attach any type of file to an email and to send more than one file at the same time.*

8 *Many computer viruses are spread via email and most email programs will check any attachment that you send or receive. If you get a warning message it is best not to open the attachment.*

9 *You can set up your own folders into which you store files.*

10 *You need to know a little bit about the libraries and folders on your computer so that you know where to find the files that you want to attach.*

10

Finding what you need on the Internet

In this chapter you will learn
- *what the Internet is*
- *how to type in a 'web address'*
- *what a hyperlink is and how to follow one*
- *how to move forward and back through web pages*
- *how to use a 'search engine'*
- *how to assess whether a website is reliable*
- *what to do when websites don't work*

10.1 What is the Internet?

The Internet is a worldwide connection of computers. It can be used for communicating and sharing information in many ways, and the most important of these is the World Wide Web. This is made up of millions and millions of pages of information, and the links between them. These pages are called web pages. A collection of web pages is called a website. All sorts of organizations and individuals might create a website.

In many cases these are businesses trying to sell things, but also include government organizations, charities, clubs and private individuals.

This presents a couple of problems. The first is that there is so much information available that it can be difficult to find what you need. The second is that there is an awful lot of rubbish in among the good stuff.

Hints and tips
The Internet or Net refers to the global connection of computers. The World Wide Web or Web refers to some of the information that is available on the Internet.

10.2 Finding a website when you know the address

The easiest way to find a website is if you know the address. Website addresses are unique, so no two websites can have exactly the same name. Most organizations advertise their web addresses and include them in their advertising. For example: www.oxfam.org.uk

Hints and tips
Internet Explorer is a web browser – software that allows you to look at websites. Internet Explorer is the most widely used but there are other web browsers available such as Mozilla Firefox, Opera and Netscape. These work in exactly the same way, but look slightly different.

To go to a website if you know the address:

1 *Double click on the 'Internet Explorer' icon from your desktop or click on the icon in Taskbar at the bottom of the screen. You can also click on the 'Start' icon and select Internet Explorer from there. This gives you three different ways of doing exactly the same thing! Internet Explorer will now load and a web page will be displayed. This is known as your home page and is always the first page to be shown. In this case, the home page is MSN®, which is the Microsoft® Net home page for the UK. Yours might be something completely different.*

2 *At the top of the page is the address bar highlighted in the image above. Type in the address – in this case www.oxfam.org.uk. It is important that you type the address exactly as shown with the correct slashes and full stops where relevant.*

3 *Press ENTER. After a few seconds, you will be taken to the page with the address that you have just typed in. When you get to the page, it is probably the home page of the website. This is the main page and should contain general information that welcomes you to the site and tells you about the organization or person who is responsible for the site.*

Once you are in the website, you may need to move to other parts of the website to find what you want. Nearly all web pages include links to other pages. These links are called hyperlinks. They might take you to another page on the same website, or to a page on another website.

Hyperlinks can be attached to anything. There might be a link from a piece of text, or from a picture. Website designers try to make it easy for you to spot the links and explain where the link will take you. Also, the mouse pointer, which normally looks like this ▷ will change when you hover it over an object on a web page. If it changes to a little hand like this ⌐ that means that there is a link to another page.

4 *Find a hyperlink (any hyperlink) and click on it. You are now taken to a different web page. This page will probably have lots of information on it, and lots more hyperlinks too.*
5 *One of the problems is that you can quite quickly lose track of where you are. After you have clicked on a few hyperlinks, you have lost the page where you started. If this happens, click the 'Back' button,*

which is the arrow pointing left as shown. This will take you to the previous page.

6 *Click the 'Back' button again. This will take you back to the page before that, and so on until eventually you are back where you started.*

Another problem is that sometimes when you click on a hyperlink, a new window opens up. This means that your original page is still open in the background. To get back to the original page in this case click on the small cross in the top right-hand corner of the window. This window then closes, and your original page is displayed again.

10.3 Structure of web addresses

It is useful to be able to recognize the way that web addresses are put together. Sometimes it will give you a hint about the nature of the site. Most addresses look like this: www.hodder.co.uk

▶ *The www means World Wide Web and most (but not all) web addresses start with this. Usually you don't even need to type this in as the browser will add it in automatically for you.*

- ▶ *The next part tells you the name of the individual or organization who owns the website. In this case it is* <u>Hodder</u> *(the publisher of this book).*
- ▶ *The last part of the address tells you what type of organization or person owns the website and where it is in the world. The list below shows some common examples.*
  - ▷ *.com Stands for 'commercial' and will be a business. Could be anywhere in the world.*
  - ▷ *.co.uk a UK business.*
  - ▷ *.org.uk a UK organization, but not a business, e.g. a charity.*
  - ▷ *.gov.uk a UK government website.*
  - ▷ *.ac.uk a UK college or university. The 'ac' is short for academic.*
  - ▷ *.au, .it, .de These are country codes that appear at the end of an address and indicate which country they come from. In this example: Australia, Italy and Germany.*

10.4 Finding information using a search engine

If you do not know the web address, you will need to search the Internet to find the information you need. To do this, you need a search engine.

Search engines are free and you can access them using the Internet. There are lots to choose from but the most common ones are Google™, Yahoo!® and Ask™. They all do the same thing and it is up to you which one you use. The most popular one at the moment is Google.

A search engine allows you to type in keywords that describe what you are looking for. For example, let's say we want to make a donation to the British Red Cross and we need to find the website. You might start by searching for: 'Charities'. It will then search through the web to find web pages that contain information based on the keywords you typed in.

When it has found all the sites, it will display them in a list. The list may take up hundreds of pages.

Hints and tips

Even the best search engine doesn't search every single page on the Internet. You might want to experiment with a couple of different search engines to find the one you like the best. The organizations that provide these search engines are commercial businesses so they will all tell you that theirs is the best.

1 *Open Internet Explorer.*
2 *Type 'www.google.co.uk' into the address bar. The Google home page will load.*
3 *Type the word 'Charity' into the box as shown in the following screenshot. You will notice that as you type, a list of possible search words will be displayed. Google is showing you common searches that are like the word you have typed in.*

*You can ignore these or if you see the words
you are looking for in the list then click on
them.*

4 *Click on the button for 'pages from the UK'.
This means that you should only get websites
based in the UK, although some others may
get through.*

5 *Click on the 'Google Search' button.*

After a few seconds it will show the results pages listing
all of the websites that contain information about
charities.

This page contains links to the first ten websites
that contain information that meet your keywords.
It also contains some sponsored links, which mean that
businesses have paid Google so that their websites will
appear on this page. These are the ones highlighted in
pink at the top and the ones down the right-hand side.

Each website shown on the results page can be opened by clicking on it. You can read what it says about the website and use this to decide whether it is worth clicking on or not.

In the top right-hand corner you will see how many pages the search engine has found. In this case it has found 24,300,000 pages. This is sometimes called the number of hits. It would take years to search through all of these, so we need to narrow down the search.

Let's narrow down the search:

1 *Type the words 'British Red Cross' into the box. You will find that this reduces the number of hits significantly, and that the website for the British Red Cross is first on the list on the first page of results.*

2 *We actually wanted to find out how to donate to the British Red Cross so we could do two things here. We could:*
3 *Click on the link to the British Red Cross website.*
4 *Follow the hyperlinks to the donation section.*

Or you could refine the search still further:

1 *Type the words: 'British Red Cross + donation' exactly as shown.*
2 *Press ENTER. The results page will now show a direct link to the donations web page of the British Red Cross website.*

Hints and tips

Putting words inside speech marks means that the search will show only websites that contain those words in that sequence. Using the + sign means that it will only include sites that also contain the word 'donation'.

10.5 How to tell if a website is trustworthy

Just because a website is listed by a search engine, does not mean that it contains the information you need, or that the information is correct. Anyone can put information onto a website and there are plenty of strange people out there!

It is not always easy to tell how reliable a website is, but there are some general guidelines you can use:

- *Rely on websites only if they are from organizations or businesses that you already know and trust.*
- *Check for an 'About Us' link to see if you can find out who is responsible for the site.*
- *Check the name of the site. If it is a .gov site for example, you know that it has come from the government (whether you trust it or not is up to you!). If it is .co.uk it could be from anyone.*
- *Most sites are trying to sell you something, so you need to be as cynical as you would be if confronted with a pushy salesperson in a shop!*
- *Some websites are what is known as secure sites. There is more information on this in Chapter 16.*

10.6 Dead links and redirection

Finally, it is quite common to click on a hyperlink and not to get the page you want. This might be for a number of reasons. The web page might no longer exist, or the link might have been set up incorrectly. These are sometimes called dead links as they don't take you anywhere. You will most likely get a message on the screen saying that the web page has not been found.

If this happens:

1 *Click on 'Back'. This will take you back to the page that you linked from. It is worth trying again, as sometimes you just get a bad connection. If you try*

again and you get the same message, then the link
is probably dead and there is nothing you can do
about it.

Sometimes you will be redirected to another website. Sometimes this is for genuine reasons, as the website may have been moved to a different address. Sometimes, it is an advertising ploy to take you to a site that then tries to sell you something. A bit like dead links, all you can do is:

2 *Click on 'Back' or click on the cross to close the window.*

10.7 Bookmarking websites

When you find a good website, you will probably want to use it over and over again. Rather than having to remember the address, or go through the search engine to find it again, you can add the website to a list of 'favourites'. This is also known as a bookmark.

Bookmarking a website means that you can get at it quickly from the menus options. In this example, we will bookmark the Oxfam site:

1 *Open Internet Explorer.*
2 *Type 'www.oxfam.org.uk' into the address bar and press ENTER.*

When the page has opened:
  3 *Click on the 'Favorites' icon from the menu at the top left of the screen and then click on 'Add to Favorites'.*
  4 *Click on 'Add' and click OK.*

If you want to go to this site at any time, all you need to do is:

  1 *Click on the 'Favorites' icon at the top left of the screen and select the Oxfam website from the list displayed.*

IMPORTANT THINGS TO REMEMBER FROM THIS CHAPTER

1 *The Internet is a worldwide connection of computers. It contains millions of web sites all made up of web pages.*

2 *Anyone with a computer and an ISP can have a web site. This means that in amongst all the good stuff on the Internet there is a lot of rubbish too.*

3 *To access the Internet you need to use browser software. The Microsoft version of this is called Internet Explorer.*

4 *All web sites have a unique web address. If you know the address you can type it into the address bar in Internet Explorer and go straight to it.*

5 *Web pages can contain of text, graphics, photos, videos, animations and sounds. They also contain hyperlinks which you click on to move to different web pages.*

6 *The address of the web site will often give you a clue as to what type of site it is. For example if it has .com, it means it is a commercial web site.*

7 *If you don't know the web address, you need to use a search engine such as Google to find what you want.*

8 *You can type search words into a search engine and it will come back with a list of web pages that match them. You need to be quite specific in your search words so that you don't get too many web sites listed.*

9 *You need to be a little wary about the information you find on some web sites. Not all web sites are trustworthy and reliable.*

10 *You can bookmark your favourite web sites to make it easier to re-visit them in the future.*

11

Buying products and services online

In this chapter you will learn
- *how to find products and services on the Internet*
- *how to buy products and services on the Internet*
- *how to compare prices*
- *how to add items into your basket*
- *how to go to an online checkout*
- *things to watch out for when buying online*

11.1 Introduction

Buying products and services over the Internet is pretty much the same as buying them from a shop – you go into the shop, browse, put things in your basket, go to the checkout and pay up. There are a few key differences, which are explained later in the chapter. You might be nervous about buying things online, as there is much talk about online fraud. Fraud does happen and you could be a victim, in much the same way as you could be in a normal shop. For specific information on keeping safe online, see Chapter 16.

11.2 Getting started

The first step is to get online and find the products that you want to buy. To do this you either need to:

▶ *Know the Internet address of the website that sells the product.*
▶ *Use a search engine to find a website that sells the product.*

There are different approaches to this. You could go to the website of a well-known retailer (e.g. Tesco, PC World) and then browse their site to find the product you want. Alternatively, you could type in the name of the product you want (e.g. Samsung DVD player, Hitachi CD player) and see what results you find for them. You could type in more general terms like 'DVD player' which would list all DVD players of all makes.

Another option is the use of comparison sites. These are websites that are set up just to compare the prices of products. They will show you all the places where you can buy the product and list the price that you will be charged.

Hints and tips
You will remember from Chapter 10 that you need to exercise some caution when using websites and you need to ensure that the site is genuine and reliable.

11.3 Finding the website of a well-known business

Many businesses that have shops also have websites, so your start point might be to find the website of a well-known retailer. For example, Tesco, Asda and Sainsbury's all have websites where you can buy the same products online as you can in the store. Currys and PC World all have online stores where you can order the same products that they have in their stores.

To find these websites:

1 *Open Internet Explorer from the desktop, the Taskbar or the 'Start' menu.*
2 *When your home page is loaded, type 'www.google.co.uk' in the address bar. You will notice that because you have been to the Google website before, you only need to type the first few letters and it will be displayed in a list. You can simply click on it from this list.*
3 *When Google opens, type 'Asda' in the box and click the 'Search Google' button.*
4 *As these businesses are so big, their website is almost bound to be the first one in the list.*
5 *Click on the link to the website from the Google results page. This takes you to the home page of the website from which you can follow the links to different sections.*

11.4 Searching for a product from a retailer

If you want to buy a specific product from a specific retailer, for example if you want a Samsung DVD player from Currys, then you should use the search function on the Currys website. If you are not fussed which retailer you buy it from, skip to the next section.

1 *In the address bar, type 'www.currys.co.uk'. This is the website of Currys, the electrical retailer.*
2 *The Currys home page will load and will look something like this although it will have changed since this book was published. You can now follow the links through the products you are looking for, or use the search option provided in the website.*

3   The links to different sections are listed down the
    left-hand side in this case. There is a link called
    'TV, DVD and Blu-ray', which you could click on.
    Alternatively, you could use the search box. In the
    box, type 'Samsung DVD' and click on 'Find'.

4   The whole of the Currys website will now be
    searched and the results will be displayed on a new
    screen as shown. In this example, the search engine
    has found 38 matches with Samsung DVD and they
    are listed.

5   Scroll down until you find the one you are
    interested in. If there are lots of results then these
    may be shown over several pages. If this is the
    case you will see a hyperlink labelled 'Next' and it
    will show you how many pages there are. In this
    example, there are four pages of results.

6 *Click on the image and you will be taken to a screen that gives you more information about the product.*

On most websites, product information usually includes a fairly detailed specification of the product and some customer reviews. These reviews are often quite useful and are usually genuine on well-known sites.

11.5 Searching for a product across the whole Web

There are some real bargains to be had on the Internet. Some retailers only sell over the Internet, and this gives them a big advantage over business with shops in that they have lower overheads in running their business. Often (but not always) this means that products from online businesses are cheaper than from shops.

As with normal shopping it is often worth shopping around. To follow through from the example before, if you want a Samsung DVD player and don't care where you buy it from, you would be better searching the whole Internet, rather than just one website.

To do this:

1 *Type 'www.google.co.uk' into the address bar in Internet Explorer. Again, as you have been to Google before you only need to type in the first few letters and it will be displayed in a list. You don't even need to type the www bit.*

2 *Type the name of the product into the box and click 'Search Google'.*
   As you saw in Chapter 10, it is better to be as precise as possible when typing in your search words. If you know you want a Samsung DVD R-130, then type that exactly to narrow down the number of hits. If you just want a Samsung DVD player, or just a DVD player of any make, then you should type in the search words accordingly.

3 *Type 'Samsung DVD R-130' into Google, click the 'pages from the UK' button and click 'Google Search'.*

4 *You can now start to look through the results and decide which links are worth following. Remember that some links are sponsored which means that businesses have paid the search engine company to put them nearer the top.*

5 *Click on a few links until you find a site that you trust. You can then complete the purchase online as described later.*

11.6 Using a price comparison site

In most cases these days, if you type in a particular product, the first few hits from the search engine will be what are called comparison sites. These websites exist purely to compare the prices of products and services. They do not actually sell the products, but will direct you to other online stores that do. Most of these are commercial websites that make their money from the suppliers that they recommend and, as such, you need to question how impartial they might be.

They will list all of the suppliers that they know of who sell that product and will show you how much it will cost and provide a link to the supplier's website. Comparison websites for financial services are very common, e.g. confused.com, comparethemarket.com, etc.

For this example we will use a comparison website that compares electrical products among other things. This is called Kelkoo™ and is one of the most popular price comparison sites in the UK.

1 *Type 'www.kelkoo.co.uk' into the address bar of Internet Explorer.*
2 *The Kelkoo home page will now load which will look something like this. Like many sites, it has its own search engine, which you can see near the top of the page where it says: 'What are you shopping for?'*

3 *Type 'Samsung DVD' and click the 'Search' button. All of the Samsung DVD products will now be listed. This may go across several pages. If this is the case you will see an option to move onto the next page either at the bottom of this page.*

4 *Locate the product you are interested in and click the 'Compare Prices' button. A new list is displayed showing all of the websites from which you can buy the product, along with the price. This is a direct comparison of the price of exactly the same product, from all of these different suppliers.*

5 *Look through the list and choose which supplier you would like to use and click on the 'Visit store' link. This will then take you directly to the website of the store.*

Hints and tips

Price comparison sites will list some suppliers that you have heard of and some that you have not. See the general advice in Chapters 10 and 16 about how to identify a legitimate supplier and how to keep safe when online. Some retailers are not listed on comparison sites so you are not guaranteed to get the best deal by using one.

11.7 Making the purchase

After you have found the product you want on a site from which you want to buy it, it is now time to complete the purchase. Most sites have a basket. This is the same as a basket in a shop i.e. you put stuff in it.

Like a shop you can put things back if you want to and it is only when you get to the checkout that you must pay for your items.

Most sites simply have an 'Add to basket' button next to every product and by clicking it, it puts it into your basket and you carry on browsing for the next item and so on. On some sites it just says 'add' and on some sites you get a little icon (picture) of a basket.

You can view the contents of your basket at any time, and add and remove items from it. All websites look slightly different, but the principle is the same. Find the link to 'View Basket' or words to that effect. The Currys basket looks like this:

The 'Remove' button does just that, and takes the item out of the basket. Most websites have 'Continue shopping' button takes you back into the shop so you can put more stuff in your basket and the 'Go to checkout' is what you do when you have finished shopping and want to pay.

1   *Click on the 'Go to checkout' option. On other sites, it might simply be called 'Checkout'. The checkout section of each website will look different but essentially they all do the same thing. You will be asked for personal details and credit or debit card details. Many sites will ask you to register, which means that they store your details. This can be handy as it means that if you buy anything from them again, they remember all the details from the last time.*

2   *Complete all of the details that they ask for. This will involve typing in your credit or debit card number. See Chapter 16 for more details on keeping yourself safe online. Filling in the details may take some time as they ask you for quite a lot of information. Follow the instructions on the screen. If you miss any bits out they will tell you.*

3   *The last stage of the checkout process is to confirm the order. At any point up to here you can simply close the window down and none of the information you have typed in will be saved. Click 'Confirm'. When you have done this you will usually be given the option of printing out an order confirmation. You will also receive an order confirmation via email within a few minutes.*

4   *Wait a day or two and the doorbell will ring, and there will be your parcel!*

11.8 Things to watch out for when buying online

The first point is related to the last one made above and that is, that you will have to wait for delivery. Many websites will deliver within a day or two, but some will take longer. Often this is because they do not have the item in stock, and have to wait for it. The best advice here is to use websites that are recommended to you by friends, or that you have used before and know to be good.

Delivery charges can sometimes be excessive and more than the actual cost of delivery. Some websites appear to offer cheap products, but then add a large delivery charge. You may not discover this until quite a long way through the ordering process. Remember, you can always click on the cross at any time if you don't like the scale of delivery charges and don't want to proceed. Also, most websites now have a scale of charges for delivery depending on how quickly you want to receive your product. You can end up paying a lot more for next day delivery.

Watch out for other hidden charges. Some websites charge VAT on top of the prices that they are quoting on their websites. So something that looks like a bargain at £99.99 with VAT and delivery to add on could cost you £137.50. It is the final order confirmation that must clearly show you what you are paying, so check this carefully before you confirm the order.

One big disadvantage of the Internet is that you can see only a picture of what you are buying – you can't see it for real. There are a couple of things you can do here. The first is a bit cheeky, but you can pop down to a shop and take a look at it in the flesh and then come home and buy it online. The second is to check whether the website offers a returns policy so that you can get your money back if you don't like the item when it arrives.

11.9 Online grocery shopping

Buying groceries online can be excellent. It can take a long time to go through and select all of the products that you want, but when you have done it once, you can edit the list each week rather than doing it from scratch. You can redeem all of your vouchers as if you were at the supermarket and best of all, someone goes round and gets it all for you and delivers it to your door.

Some retailers will not charge you extra for this service and some make a small charge. If you live a distance from the supermarket this can represent good value as it saves you time and money. However, all retailers do put a limit on how far they will deliver.

Again, ask around among your friends, as some retailers are better than others. For example, do they deliver within the stated time slot, what do they do if the product you want is out of stock, do they select the best fruit and vegetables or the grotty ones off the floor?

IMPORTANT THINGS TO REMEMBER FROM THIS CHAPTER

1 *Buying goods and services over the Internet is much the same as buying them in shops and many of the same rules apply.*

2 *You can find many well-known high street shops on the Internet too.*

3 *You can use a search engine to search for particular products or retailers.*

4 *Most web sites are organized so that you can either browse through at a range of products within a category or search for specific items.*

5 *You can often find deals on the Internet that are not available in stores.*

6 *Price comparison sites allow you to compare the price of the same product or service from a range of different suppliers.*

7 *Web sites have a check out, just like a normal shop. You can pay using your debit or credit card, or other online payment methods.*

8 *You may have to pay a delivery charge on top of the price and you will have to wait for delivery.*

9 *You should shop around and take advice from your family and friends the same as you would when buying from a normal shop.*

10 *Grocery shopping is available in most areas and is an easy way to shop, though there may be a delivery charge.*

12

Buying from an online auction

In this chapter you will learn
* *how to set up an eBay account*
* *how to search and browse for products*
* *how to place a bid*
* *how to pay for your product*
* *things to watch out for using eBay.*

12.1 Introduction

eBay™ is currently the world's biggest online auction site boasting more than 230 million users worldwide with millions of items for sale at any one time.

It works much in the same way as a traditional auction in that items are offered for sale, you look at them and read the description, and then decide whether you want to bid on the item or not. Many other people will be doing the same thing and bidding against you. The big difference with a real auction is the period of time over which the bidding takes place, as it can be several days.

At the end of this period, if your bid is the highest, you win. You then pay for the product and the seller sends it to you, or you go and pick it up.

Although eBay was originally intended for items of relatively low value, it is now possible to buy virtually anything on eBay including cars, holidays and even houses.

12.2 Getting started

First, you need to register. To do this, you must already have an email address. If you do not have one, refer to Chapter 8.

1 *Open Internet Explorer either from the desktop, the Taskbar or the 'Start' menu.*
2 *In the address bar, type 'www.ebay.co.uk'. (eBay operates in more than 30 countries, so make sure that you use the correct version for the country that you are in.) The opening page is displayed and will look something like this.*
3 *Click on the 'Register' button. You now have to fill in a form. This will ask you for your personal details and email contact details. You will also be asked to think of a user ID and password, which you will need to use every time you log on to eBay.*
4 *Complete the form. This may take a few minutes.*
5 *Make a note of your user ID and remember your password.*

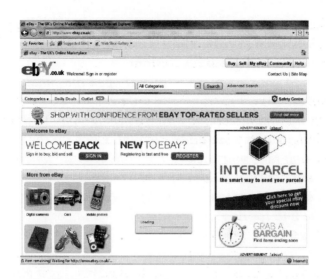

12. **Buying from an online auction** 159

6 *When you have completed the form, you will be sent an email from eBay. This is an automatic process and should be instant.*

7 *Go to your email account and open the email from eBay.*

8 *In the email, you are asked to click on a link that will activate your eBay account. Click on the link. It will take you back to the eBay website where you can now start bidding for products.*

9 *To make sure you are in the 'Buy' section, click on the link to 'Buy' in the top right-hand corner of the page:*

12.3 Finding what you want

There are two ways to find the items you are looking for:

▶ *You can browse, which means you can look through a wide range of products under certain categories.*

▶ *You can search, which means you type in a few keywords that describe the item you want and it will search through all the items and display only those items that match the description you have typed in.*

BROWSING FOR AN ITEM

If you do not specifically know what you want, then browsing through the eBay categories is the best option.

For example, if you want to look at antique chairs, but do not have a specific item in mind:

1 *Look through the categories until you find the one you want. In this case, it will be under 'Antiques' so click on this link. You are now presented with a more detailed list of categories within the Antiques section.*
2 *Under Antique Furniture click on 'Chairs'.*

3 *You are now at the screen that lists all of the items that are for sale under this category. In this example, there are 3048 items for sale. To view the entire list of items for sale, you need to scroll down. It is not possible to show all 3048 items on one page, so at the bottom of the first page, there are links to several other pages.*
4 *On the left-hand side of each page, you will see that there are further subcategories for the type, age or style of the chair. For example, there are categories*

for 'Dining Chairs', 'Armchairs', etc. This will
help you to narrow down your search reducing the
number of items listed.

Hints and tips

It would take you hours to view all 3048 items
in this example so it would be better to try to
narrow down the search, if you can, using the
subcategories.

SEARCHING FOR AN ITEM

The preferred method of finding what you want on
eBay is to type in a few keywords that describe it.
As you saw in the previous section, browsing through
categories can be time-consuming as there are often so
many items for sale.

1 *Click on the 'Buy' button again to take you back
   to the main buying page where all the categories
   are listed. At the top of this page, there is a 'Search'
   box. This example will show you how to search for
   a specific item, a garden hammock.*
2 *Click in the 'Search' box and type: 'Garden
   hammock'. You can narrow down the search by
   searching only within a category using the box to
   the right of the search box.*
3 *In the 'In this category' box, which currently reads
   'All categories', select 'Home & Garden'. If you do
   not know which category something fits in to, you
   can just leave this box set to 'All categories'.*

4 *Click on 'Search'. After a few seconds, you will be presented with a list of all the garden hammocks that are currently for sale.*

12.4 Selecting your item

Once you have located an item that you are interested in, you need to get a few more details about it and the seller. In the first instance you need to know the price, how many bids there are on it, and how long there is left on the auction.

The screen listing all of the items gives you some useful information to help you decide whether to look in more detail at the item.

These are:

▶ **Photograph** *of the product – the seller puts this on. If there isn't a photograph, be suspicious.*
▶ **Item Title** *– a brief description put on by the seller.*
▶ **Bids** *– shows you the number of people who have put in a bid on this item. If it is displaying the 'Buy It Now' symbol it means that it you must pay the price quoted, you cannot bid for it. Other option in here are 'Buy it Now or Best Offer', which means they are open to offers and 'Classified', which means it is an advert like the ones you get in the back of your local paper.*
▶ **Price** *– the highest price currently bid or the asking price if it is a 'Buy it now' item.*

▶ **Postage** – *how much the seller will charge you to send the item. Keep an eye out for over-the-top charges.*

▶ **Time Left** – *how many days or hours there are left until the auction closes. When the auction closes, the highest bidder at that point wins.*

This information is displayed for every item that is for sale. If you are still interested in the item you can now find out more about it and the seller.

12.5 Finding out more about the items and the seller

To view more details about any specific item:

1 *Click on the photograph or on the item title. This then displays a further page that gives you details about the product, usually some more photographs and the seller rating, which gives you an idea of how reliable the seller is.*

2 *A fuller description of the product can be obtained by scrolling down the page. On the right-hand side is a seller rating. When people buy items from eBay they are asked to rate the seller and make comments about them. You can view these comments and read the ratings by following these links. It will show you the number of people who have commented and provide an overall rating. In this example, the*

seller has *575 ratings and they are all positive giving
a 100% rating.*

3 *You can contact the seller direct to ask about the
product or delivery arrangements, etc. This is
advisable on larger value items in particular.*

Hints and tips

eBay provides useful hints and tips about trading
on their website. For example, this page in the
diagram above has a link to a section on safe
buying tips.

12.6 Making a bid

Once you have found the item you want, you can bid
on it. If either of the 'Buy It Now' options or 'Classified
Ad' logos are shown, you can just buy it at this point

without having to bid at all or contact the seller with an offer. Assuming that bidding is required:

1 *From the current screen, click on the 'Place Bid' button.*
2 *This will take you to a screen where you can type in how much you want to bid. A useful feature here is that you can type in the maximum amount you are prepared to pay and eBay will automatically keep increasing your bid, if you are out-bid by someone else. If the price goes beyond your maximum bid, it will stop bidding and you will not win the auction.*

3 *Finally, you are asked to confirm the bid. It is at this point that you are entering a legal contract to buy the item. So if you win, you must buy it. Only click on continue if you want to buy the item!*
4 *The next step is to keep an eye on the bidding from time to time, or just wait until the time runs out and*

see whether you have won. eBay has a feature called 'My eBay'. You can opt to 'Watch this item', which means that it will put the item you are interested in into a list for you, where you can watch the progress of the bidding. To do this, from the item's description screen like the one shown, click on 'Watch this item'.

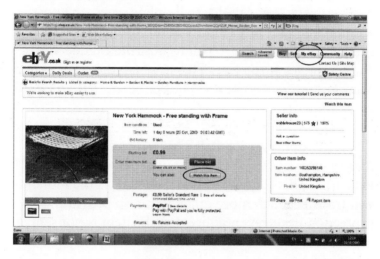

5 *To view the 'My eBay' area, click on 'My eBay' near the top of the screen. The hammock is listed here and it is possible to view the bidding as it progresses.*

12.7 Winning and paying

When you win an auction for an item or if you opt to 'Buy It Now' you need to pay for the item. If you win or lose an auction, you will be informed by email. There are different ways of paying. You are supplied with contact details of the seller. This is often just an email address or maybe a phone number. If this is the case, you could just contact the seller and make arrangements like any other buying/selling arrangement.

Alternatively, you can do it all online or via the post with no need for any contact at all. Many sellers accept cheques but will require you to post the cheque and allow time for it to clear. This is where the seller rating is important, as you need to be confident that you will receive the item.

The other option is PayPal. This is a free and secure service where you pay using your credit or debit card via email. This is quicker than a cheque as the money will transfer much more quickly. It also provides protection in the eventuality that the item is not sent, or that it is significantly different from the way it was described.

To use PayPal you will need to register with the PayPal website first. This process is similar to registering for eBay in the first place and can be done by following the links to PayPal from the eBay site or by typing 'www.paypal.co.uk' into the address bar and then clicking on the 'Sign Up Now' link.

Once you have done this you will be able to use this method wherever the seller accepts PayPal. You will receive an email confirming your order, and you click on the 'Pay Now' option.

12.8 Things to watch out for using eBay

In common with anything else on the Internet, there are plenty of dodgy people out there who might try to rip you off. The anonymous nature of the Internet perhaps makes this a bit easier for these people. The best advice is to use the seller ratings to make a judgement about how reliable someone might be.

Decide how much you want to spend and stick to it. In common with traditional auctions, it can be tempting to keep upping the price that you are willing to pay, only to regret it later. Many bidders leave it until the last minute to make their bids; so don't get caught up in a bidding war.

Make sure you are aware of all the charges that will be added. Keep an eye on postage costs and VAT. Many businesses now use eBay as their main way of selling products, and they will have to add on VAT. Also, make sure that the item is for sale in your country, or you may have to pay additional shipping costs and tax.

Finally, eBay™ has become an international phenomenon and as a result, there is a lot of information written about it. A good starting point is the company's own Help centre, which can be accessed by clicking the 'Help' tab on their home page.

IMPORTANT THINGS TO REMEMBER FROM THIS CHAPTER

1 *eBay is the biggest auction site on the Internet. On it you can buy and sell anything from old rope to houses.*

2 *You have to register with eBay if you want to buy or sell anything.*

3 *In common with other web sites where you can buy things, there is a browse option and a search option to help you find what you want.*

4 *There is quite a lot of information about products and their sellers. You should read all of this to make sure you know what you are bidding on.*

5 *All sellers have a rating and feedback left by previous buyers. You should check to see whether previous buyers have had any problems.*

6 *You can bid on the items you want to buy on an ongoing basis or you can put in a maximum bid.*

7 *There is a 'watch this item' feature which allows you to keep an eye on certain auctions whether you are bidding on them or not.*

8 *If you win you will be notified by email and you will have to pay by card, cheque or PayPal. The seller will stipulate what payment methods they accept.*

9 *There may be some dodgy people using eBay so you need to exercise the same caution that you would with any other kind of purchase.*

10 *Auctions run for a set number of days. There is a count down on each item so you can see how long is left. Many bidders leave it until very late to place a bid.*

13

Communicating with other people using the Internet

In this chapter you will learn
- *how to use the Internet to keep in touch*
- *how to use chat rooms*
- *how to access newsgroups*
- *how to make phone calls over the Internet*
- *how to make video calls over the Internet*

13.1 Introduction

When your computer is connected to the Internet, you are part of a massive collection of computers all communicating with each other. It is possible to communicate using text, voice and video with anybody who is connected.

There are several ways of doing this, some of which require special software, most of which is free from the Internet. However, to access most of these efficiently, you will need a broadband line, otherwise the connection may be too slow.

13.2 Chat rooms

An Internet chat room is a 'virtual' room where people can enter and talk about anything they like. Chat rooms normally have a specific theme, for example you might enter a chat room to discuss politics, or the news, or computers. There are hundreds of chat rooms to choose from on the Internet. Many chat rooms exist for dating purposes or for chat of an 'adult' nature so you need to be sure about what type of room you are entering. It is usually pretty obvious from the website as to what type of chat room you are going into. If you don't like it, just click on the cross and leave.

This example will look at the chat rooms provided by Orange, which is a well-known mobile phone network.

Hints and tips
There are lots of dodgy chat rooms out there. Only use chat rooms from well-known and reliable websites.

1 *Open Internet Explorer from the desktop, the Taskbar or the Start menu.*
2 *In the address bar, type www.orange.co.uk/ communicate/chat/main. The main Orange chat page is now displayed.*

3 On this page you can see that there are three main
   categories for teenagers, general and adult chat. As
   you can see, some of the rooms are based on topics
   such as politics or art, some are based on where
   people live and some on age. You can enter into any
   of these rooms once you have registered and start
   chatting to see what you think. If you don't like it
   or the room has no-one in then you simply leave
   and try another one.

4 When you select a room for the first time you will be
   asked to register and – you guessed it – fill in a form.

5 Fill in the form and click on 'Register'. In common
   with some other websites, you need to put your
   email address in.

6 *After you have completed the form you will be sent an email from the website, which you need to open in order to activate your account. You will need to check you emails now. You should have one sent by Orange. Open it and follow the instructions. This will take you to the chat page, which will look like this:*

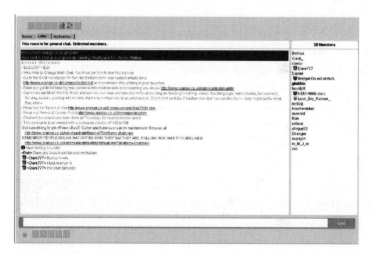

7 *On the right-hand side you can see the chat names of everyone who is currently in this room. To start chatting, simply type in what you want to say and press ENTER or click 'Send'. Whatever you have written will appear in the main window next to your name. Other people will now respond to you and you can start chatting.*

8 *You may get an offer of a 'PC' or 'Personal Chat'. This means that the person wants to speak one-to-one with you and no-one else will be able to see what you are chatting about. You can accept or decline this offer.*

9 *To change to a different room, click on the tab labelled 'Rooms'. You will now see a list of all the different rooms that are available and you can choose to enter any of these by clicking on it. You then carry on chatting as before with whoever is in this room. Notice that it shows you how many people are in each room.*

There are hundreds of chat rooms available and some are better than others. Orange regulates some of its chat rooms to get rid of undesirable people. Some chat rooms don't. You need to exercise some caution here. Many well-known websites have a 'chat' option, which will work in a way similar to the Orange chat rooms. Another factor is that some websites are specific to one country while others are global. You might find yourself in a chat room, therefore, where you do not speak the language.

> **Hints and tips**
> Every time you fill in a form on the Internet there is a chance that it will lead to you getting emails from these people. Just so you know.

13.3 Forums

A forum is like an online notice board where people can post messages or questions and respond to messages that others have posted. It is a bit like a chat room, but it is not live. There are literally thousands of different forums on the go at any time covering every imaginable topic.

If you are looking for a forum on a particular topic then the best bet would be to use a search engine such as Google to find one. In this example, we will look at a typical forum relating to gardening.

1 *Open Internet Explorer and type '*<u>www.gardenerscorner.co.uk/forum</u>*' into the address bar.*

2 *This will load the forum page. Most forums allow you to read messages but ask you to register if you want to leave messages. Some, but not many, make a small charge for access to a forum.*

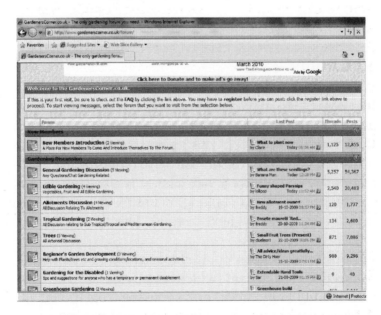

3 *In this example you can see all of the topics for discussion, which are sometimes called threads. You can click on any of these and read the messages that have been left there.*

4 *If you are looking for something in particular, find the search box and type in the keywords for whatever it is you want e.g. 'blackspot + tomatoes'.*

5 *Once you are registered with the forum (yes –another form to fill in!) you will be able to post messages yourself. The idea is that you post a message and someone will respond and a thread develops, which is an ongoing list of messages and responses.*

6 *To respond to a message, go to the bottom of the message and click on the 'Reply' button, and type in your message and click 'Send'.*

7 *Click on the cross when complete.*

13.4 Phone calls

It is possible to make telephone calls over the Internet using something called VOIP, which stands for Voice Over Internet Protocol. This means that you can talk into your computer to someone else on his or her computer. If you have a web cam, it is also possible to see the person you are talking to and for them to see you (this is covered in the next section). This service is free.

For this to work, you do need a broadband Internet connection, a web cam (which usually has a microphone built into it) and some speakers. If you think you might use this a lot, you could buy an internet phone or headset which plug into your USB port. You may need to go back to Chapter 2 to find out how to add these to your computer system if you do not have them already.

There are different websites where you can download VOIP. This section will be using a popular one called Skype™.

First, you will need to download the Skype software onto your computer. You will also need to have someone with a computer and Skype at the other end so you have got someone to talk to.

1 *Open Internet Explorer.*
2 *Type 'www.skype.com' into the address bar. The Skype home page will now open.*
3 *Click on the links to 'download' and select 'Run' when prompted. The software will then start to download. You will see a screen that looks like this:*

This is the first example in this book of having to download software from the Internet. We discussed this briefly in Chapter 5.

4 *It may take a few minutes to download the software. When the download is complete, click 'Run'.*

5 *Another screen will now be displayed. You will need to click to accept the terms of the licence and then click 'OK'. The main Skype screen will now be displayed. As with chat rooms and forums you must first register, which means choosing a name and password.*

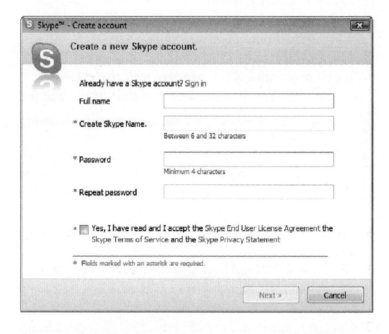

6 *Complete the form making a note of the 'Skype Name' that you have chosen. You need to tick to accept the terms and conditions again and you will be asked for your email address.*

7 *Click on 'Next' and proceed to use Skype. It will take a couple of minutes to create your account. The following screen is displayed. It is probably worth spending a bit of time reading the 'See what Skype can do for you' section and checking that your web cam, microphone or internet phone are working properly.*

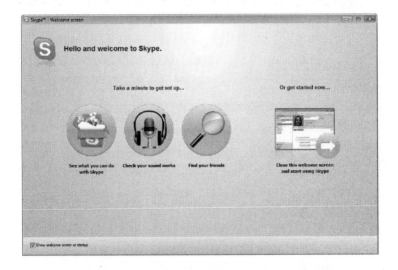

8 *Click on 'Close this welcome screen and start using Skype'.*

9 *Click on the 'New' button and select 'New contact' and type in the Skype Name of the person you want to contact.*

10 *Click on 'Find' and it will search for that person in its own directory. If it can't find the name you will get a message and you will have to try again.*

11 *Once the contact has been found, click on the name and then click on the green 'Call icon'. The software will then dial that person as if you were on the phone.*

12 *If they are online, they will answer and you will
hear their voice coming out of your speakers or
internet phone. You can now talk to them as if it
were a normal phone call. If they are not online
then you will get a message saying it could not
connect. If it just rings and rings it means that the
person is not near their computer.*

13 *To end the call, click on the red phone symbol at
the bottom.*

If someone calls you using Skype, you will hear your
computer ringing and you will need to click on the
green phone symbol to accept the call.

Note that you can also send text messages by clicking
on the 'Conversations' tab. If the person is on-line
they will get the message instantly and can reply. This

is known as 'instant messaging'. If they are not on-line the message will stay there and they will see it next time they load their Skype software. If anyone sends you a message you will see that the tab goes orange.

13.5 Video calls

Once you have established a voice connection, you will be given the option to video call with that person if you both have web cams set up on your computer.

1 *Select 'Call' from the menu across the top and select 'Video call'.*

If you have a webcam and the person that you are calling has a webcam, you should automatically be able see them on the screen. They will be able to see you too. If you cannot see them, or they cannot see you:

2 *Select 'Tools' from the menu across the top.*
3 *Select 'Options'.*
4 *Select 'Video settings' from the list of options on the left-hand side.*
5 *Make sure the 'Enable Skype Video' box is ticked.*
6 *Make sure the 'Start my video automatically' box is ticked.*
7 *Click 'Save'.*
8 *You should now be able to see the person you are talking to.*

Hints and tips

Sending and receiving video images and sound requires broadband Internet speeds. Even with broadband, the sound may break up a bit, or the images may be jerky.

IMPORTANT THINGS TO REMEMBER FROM THIS CHAPTER

1 *There are lots of different ways of using the Internet to communicate with other people.*

2 *You can use the Internet to communicate with people you know and to make contact with new people through online communities.*

3 *Chat rooms are web sites where you can get together with other Internet users to send each other instant messages.*

4 *Some chat rooms are moderated, which means that someone makes sure all the chat is appropriate. Many are unmoderated and anything goes.*

5 *A forum is like an online notice board where people can post messages and questions and others can reply to them.*

6 *Forums do not happen in real time so it may take a few days or weeks for people to respond to any messages that you post up on it.*

7 *It is possible to make free phone calls over the Internet. This is called VOIP and one of the biggest providers is Skype.*

8 *You need to register with Skype, which means filling in an online form.*

9 *Once you have set up a Skype account you can call anyone else on Skype for free and talk to them using an Internet phone or headset.*

10 *It is possible to have video phone calls using Skype. You will need a web cam. This way you can be seen and heard by the other person.*

14

....

Accessing music, film, radio and TV over the Internet

In this chapter you will learn
- *the basics of accessing music, film, radio and TV using the Internet*
- *the software needed to get access to music and TV called 'players'*
- *the difference between legal and illegal content*
- *the difference between 'live' and 'download' services*
- *how to download music and film*

14.1 Introduction

Multimedia material (that's sound, images and text) is what the Internet is all about. Over recent years there has been a massive increase in the use of the Internet for viewing and listening to films, TV programmes, radio stations and music in general. The growth in the use of multimedia is because more and more people now have broadband Internet access, which means that it is accessible much more quickly than before.

> **Hints and tips**
> If you do not have broadband Internet access, you will find accessing music and film very slow indeed.

There is a mixture of things on offer. You can view current TV programmes and listen to live radio. You can download music and films, which means that you save it onto your own computer so you can watch/listen again and again. There are two problems:

▶ *There is so much of it about at the moment that it is often hard to find what you want.*
▶ *A lot of the material on offer is illegal because the websites offering it do not own the copyright.*

14.2 Getting started

If you want to listen to or view multimedia content then you will need a piece of software called a player or media player. There are lots of different players to choose from. Some of them are free. Two common ones are called Windows Media Player, which you will probably already have, and one called RealPlayer™, which you can download from the Internet. All players basically work in the same way – they let you play sounds and movies.

This chapter assumes will use Windows Media Player as it is likely that it is already installed and ready to use on your computer. There should be an icon for it in the Windows Taskbar at the bottom of the screen that looks like this.

You will also need a pair of speakers plugged into your computer. Most computers have an internal speaker, but this is very quiet, so it is recommended that you get some external speakers. You will also need a broadband Internet connection.

14.3 Listening to live radio

A Google search will show you that there are hundreds of live radio stations available over the Internet. Some a free and some are paid-for services. Some of these will be better than others. This section will show you how to access the BBC radio stations.

1 *Open Internet Explorer from the desktop, from the Taskbar or the Start menu.*
2 *In the address bar, type 'www.bbc.co.uk/radio'. This is the home page for the radio section of the BBC website. All of the radio stations are listed on this page, with links that allow you to listen live to each station.*

3 For example, to listen to Radio 2, find the link to Radio 2 and click on it. It will show you what is playing now and you can click on link to 'Listen live'. Alternatively, you can click on 'Listen again', which then gives you access to programmes that have already been on.

4 After a few seconds, the media player software will open and it will start to play. With BBC websites the player is called the BBC iPlayer. This is used to listen to radio or watch TV. Make sure your speakers are switched on at this point! The media player will be shown in a new window.

5 You can now minimize this window and continue listening to the radio while you carry on doing other things on your computer.

To stop listening:
  ▷ *Click on the cross to close the window.*
  A message will ask you if you are sure,
  click 'Yes'.

14.4 Watching TV programmes

Like the radio stations, you will also find that there
are hundreds of TV stations available on the Internet.
Again, some of these will be truly awful and some
might be worth tuning in to. Some websites will allow
you to watch for free while others make a charge.
Often, you will get snippets of programmes for free
and you have to pay for the whole programme. Some
stations, like the BBC, will allow you to watch whole
programmes for free, sometimes live and sometimes
using the 'watch again' feature, which makes the
programme available for a limited time – usually up to
a week after the programme was aired on normal TV.

The media player used to listen to radio is also used to watch TV and movies. The media player software knows automatically whether it is radio or movie and will display it accordingly.

This section will show you how to access TV programmes available on the BBC website.

1 *Open Internet Explorer from the desktop, Taskbar or the Start menu.*

2 *In the address bar, type www.bbc.co.uk/tv. This is the home page for the TV section of the BBC website. It contains links to the various BBC channels. Unlike the radio, you cannot view all of the programmes live, but there are some available.*

3 *For example, to view the BBC news channel: type 'News channel' into the search box at the top of the screen.*

4 *Click 'BBC News Channel' from the results displayed. After a few seconds, the player software will load automatically in a new window and you will be able to watch the news.*

5 *To close, simply click on the cross in the top right-hand corner of the window.*

It is exactly the same process if you want use the 'watch again' feature. Find the programme you want to watch either by typing it into the search box or by clicking on links to it when you see them. The iPlayer will then play the programme for you.

14.5 Downloading music and film

Downloading is the process of saving files from the Internet onto your own computer so that you can use them again and again. With the radio and TV that you have viewed, you have to be on the BBC website to be able to do it. If you download music and video, you have the file that contains it on your computer and you can load it at any time.

There is an awful lot of music and film available on the Internet. As with anything else on the Internet, some of it is rubbish and some of it may not be legal. Legal download sites will charge you for downloading files, illegal ones will not.

There are genuine free downloads available but unfortunately there is no way of telling whether sites are genuine or not. As a rule, if it's free and it's on a website that you have never heard of, it is probably illegal. To be on the safe side, you should always pay for your downloads unless they are from a well-known site.

This section will show you how to access a genuine legal download service using iTunes™. This is free software from Apple, the people who make the iPod™ music player. The iTunes software allows you to browse for music and video of different genre (it's not all pop music) and then download and pay for it online. You do not have to have an iPod to be able to use iTunes.

If you do not already have the iTunes software you will need to download it:

1 *Open Internet Explorer from the desktop, Taskbar or the Start menu.*
2 *In the address bar, type www.apple.com*
3 *Follow the link to 'iPod + iTunes'.*
4 *Follow the link to 'Download iTunes'.*
5 *You will need to type in your email address and then click the 'Download' button.*

Hints and tips

This is quite a big file and will take several minutes to download. If you have an iPod, this software will be in the box on a CD so it would be quicker to use that.

Once the iTunes software is downloaded:

1 *Open the iTunes software either by double clicking on the icon from the desktop or selecting it from the Start menu.*
2 *Make sure that the 'iTunes Store' is selected by clicking on it on the left-hand side. From here you can access a range of downloads including music, movies, and audio books. It will load up the pop music pages, which you may or may not want.*
3 *To select different music types, select the 'Choose Genre' option and select what you want from the list.*
4 *You can now browse through the site. This is exactly the same as the online shopping that you did in Chapter 11.*

Once you have found what you want, you can click on the option to buy it. As with all online purchases you will have to register your details and type in your credit or debit card details.

When you buy a movie or album it will then be sent direct over the Internet and you will be able to access it in the iTunes software. To do this:

1 *Click on 'Library' on the left-hand side of the iTunes software. This will list all of your downloads. To play them:*
2 *Find the one you want and double click on it. It will then start to play.*

14.6 Other download websites

There are many websites to choose from and they change daily. iTunes is one option. Whichever one you choose they all work in a similar way, although it may take a while to find the options.

In this chapter, you have used Windows Media Player and we have mentioned RealPlayer, which are two of the most common. Both of these have links in their software to online stores where you can buy music and video. The advantage of using iTunes, Windows Media Player or RealPlayer is that you can be sure that they are legal sites.

14.7 Common features of media player software

All media players allow you to select which files you want to play, be it music or film. They all have controls on them that allow you to control the file being played. These are similar to the controls you would get on a real CD or DVD player. They allow you to Play, Pause, Rewind, Fast Forward and Stop.

Luckily, there are standard symbols for these controls. This diagram shows the symbols from Windows Media® Player.

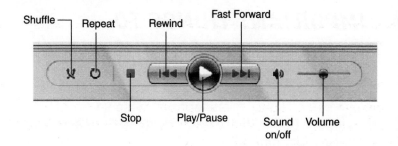

You can stop the file playing at any time and close the software, by clicking on the cross in the top right-hand corner of the window.

IMPORTANT THINGS TO REMEMBER FROM THIS CHAPTER

1 *The Internet is increasingly being used to access music, film and TV.*

2 *In addition to the usual suppliers of TV and radio programs there are hundreds of online stations.*

3 *You need software to listen to or view music, TV and video. Media Player comes with Windows and there are other players available for free.*

4 *All the big TV companies have their own media players built in to their web sites.*

5 *You can listen to live radio and use 'listen again' to catch up on programmes you have missed. There are hundreds of free radio stations to choose from, including some that cater for very specific tastes.*

6 *TV works in a similar way with some programmes shown live and some shown after they have been aired in TV.*

7 *Most broadcasters typically leave programmes up for seven days for people to listen again.*

8 *You can listen to and download all forms of music, and massive archives are available including music that can be hard to get via traditional shops.*

9 *There is a lot of music available for free, but mainstream music tends to be charged for. You should always use legal download sites.*

10 *Once you have downloaded music you can access it from your computer without having to be on the Internet.*

15

Other common uses of the Internet

In this chapter you will learn
- *how to do your banking online*
- *how to book a holiday*
- *how to find transport information*
- *how to get access to government information*
- *how to get access to local information*
- *how to trace your family tree*

15.1 Introduction

Once you start to use the Internet you realize that there are only a few basic skills that you need to get to grips with. For example:

- ▶ *using a search engine such as Google*
- ▶ *scrolling through web pages*
- ▶ *finding and clicking on links*
- ▶ *using the Forward and Back buttons*
- ▶ *filling in online forms*

Once you have done these few things, the World (Wide Web) is your oyster.

The content of the Internet is changing continually. New websites are created, are changed, or deleted all the time. New Internet crazes come and go. At the time of writing, for example, blogging and social networking are both very popular. A blog is a web log, or diary. People keep these online and let other people read them. Social networking includes websites such as Facebook, MySpace and Twitter where you can tell other people about yourself and keep in touch. If you want to find out more about either of these, then just type 'blog' or 'social networking' into an Internet search engine and off you go. In fact, if you want to find out about anything, just type it into a search engine and off you go.

In Chapters 10 to 14, you looked at how the Internet could be used for online shopping, using auction sites and communicating with others. Other common uses are listed below.

15.2 Online banking

Online banking has become increasingly popular in recent years. You can do virtually everything that you can do in a normal bank with the exception of paying real money and cheques in, and getting real money out. You can view your accounts, transfer money, pay bills, set up direct debits and standing orders, and view statements. You have access to your bank at all times.

All of the major banks offer an online service, so you can still use your branch or post office for certain transactions if you want to. Some banks are only Internet based.

Security is a serious consideration so you are advised to read the guidance notes on how to keep your personal information safe in Chapter 16, and to deal only with a reputable and well-known bank.

You will have to complete an online registration form and in order to access your account, every time you log on you will be asked for the sort code, account number, a security code, and a secret question to make it virtually impossible for anyone else to get into your account.

15.3 Booking holidays

The process of booking a holiday is the same as any other online purchase. You find the one you want, complete the form online and make a payment online using a credit card. There are some bargains to be had from buying online.

All of the same advice applies here as with any other online purchase. Make sure you know whom you are dealing with (all major travel agents have websites as well as shops) and make sure that the payment is made securely.

15.4 Transport information

You can use the Internet to check train times and book tickets, or for maps and directions, or even to get up-to-date traffic information.

For train times and tickets, try www.nationalrail.co.uk or www.thetrainline.com. Both are private companies. Both websites are owned by different groups of train and transport companies and both offer a similar service. You type in where you want to go and when and a search engine goes off and searches its database and comes back with the details of the departure and arrival times and the routes. You can also buy your ticket online.

For road information, you can try www.theaa.com or www.rac.co.uk. Both have a free route-planning feature, which allows you to type in where you are departing from and where you want to go to. You can do this using place names or postcodes. It will then produce a map and a detailed route, both of which you can print out and take with you. Both sites also have up-to-date traffic reports.

If you just want a map, then try www.multimap.co.uk which has online maps. You type in a location and it will show you a map of the area. You can zoom in and out of the map as required.

15.5 Government information

The government has policies about providing access to public information. Much of it is now available online. Government websites are identified by the .gov at the end of the address.

A good place to start is www.direct.gov.uk – this is what is called a portal site, which means that it is a central point that links lots of other websites together. So in theory, from this site, you can access all of the government websites and web pages of which there are thousands and thousands (see the next screenshot).

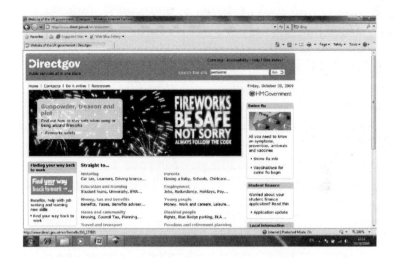

You can now either follow the various hyperlinks from this page, or use the search box in the top right-hand corner. For example, to find information on pensions:

1 *Type 'Pensions' into the search box and click 'Go'.*

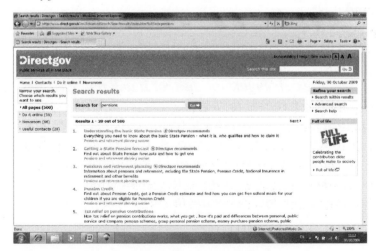

2 *A list of all pages relating to pensions is now displayed. This is a bit like a results page that Google would produce.*

3 *Scan through and click on the links that you think are relevant to what you want to find.*

4 *If the page you have linked to does not give you what you need, click 'Back' and try another link.*

You can also do things like pay for your TV licence (www.tvlicensing.co.uk) or car tax (www.direct.gov.uk/taxdisc).

15.6 Local government information

There is an abundance of local government information available. This is usually provided through websites maintained by your county council. Each county council will have its own website, so the easiest way to find it is:

1 *Type, for example, "Lincolnshire County Council" into a search engine. The use of the double quotes in a search engine means that it will find websites with references to those words, as a phrase. So instead of finding any website with any reference to Lincolnshire or County or Council, it will find websites with reference to Lincolnshire County Council. Type in your council name like this and it will come up first in the list of results.*

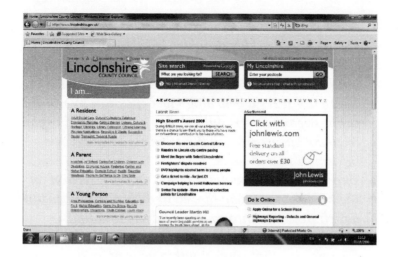

2 *You can now follow the links to find what you are interested in or by using the search box.*

Hints and tips

Although there are no rules about how websites should look, you will find that many websites share common features.

15.7 Tracing your family tree

There is a lot of information now available that will help you if you are trying to trace your family tree. Information and services are offered by government websites, some not-for-profit groups and organizations, and of course, lots of commercial websites that will charge you for their services.

- *A good place to start is www.nationalarchives. gov.uk/census. This provides links to all of the censuses that are currently available and provides links to useful advice about tracing your family tree.*
- *There are several genealogy websites run by not-for-profit organizations online. Try www.genuki.org.uk or www.silversurfers.net/interests-genealogy for information and links.*
- *The BBC also provides a family history section on their website at www.bbc.co.uk/history/familyhistory which provides information, advice and links.*
- *Also bear in mind that you will find plenty of forums and chat rooms with a genealogy theme, which you can use and communicate with other people who will be able to pass on hints and tips.*

IMPORTANT THINGS TO REMEMBER FROM THIS CHAPTER

1 *Once you have got to grips with the basic skills of the Internet such as searching and clicking on links, you can start to access anything you like.*

2 *The Internet is now being used for lots of things that traditionally used to be non-computer-based activities such as banking and shopping.*

3 *Online banking allows you to do almost everything that you can do in a high street branch.*

4 *Some people have concerns over safety but more and more people are now banking online.*

5 *Booking holidays lends itself to the Internet as the latest deals can be shown very quickly and you can snap up a bargain.*

6 *There are loads of transport and travel information and services on the Internet including booking train tickets and working out travel routes.*

7 *A number of mapping services are available on the Internet including local street mapping software that is free to use.*

8 *The government is increasingly making information available online, ranging from government policies to useful information on pensions.*

9 *Local government information is also available with all councils having their own websites where you can find access to local services.*

10 *You can use the Internet to trace you family tree. A range of free and paid-for services are available.*

16

··

Keeping safe online

In this chapter you will learn
- *what risks are involved when using the Internet*
- *how you can protect yourself against these risks*
- *advice on buying online*
- *advice on passwords*

16.1 Introduction

The Internet is a global connection of computers with the connections being made by telephone cables and satellites. It all works like the telephone system and logging on to the Internet is a bit like making a telephone call. In fact, your computer has its own number (called an IP address), which is transmitted whenever you are online.

The Internet is subject to very little regulation in this country, and pretty much anyone can get access to it. Unfortunately this means that it is open to abuse. This chapter lists the threats that exist and, in each case, explains what you can do about them.

16.2 Identity theft

Identify theft occurs when someone obtains personal information about you which means that they can pretend to be you, usually for fraudulent reasons. They could buy things from the Internet in your name, or perhaps borrow money or even clear out your bank account.

There are a number of ways that they can obtain the information:

PHISHING

This is where someone sends you an email claiming to be from your bank. They will ask for personal information, or direct you to a fake website that asks you for personal information. These emails can look very convincing.

What to do about it:

▶ *Banks will never email you to ask you for personal information such as PIN codes and passwords. If you are asked for it, don't give it.*
▶ *Make sure that when you are doing any banking over the Internet that the site is secure. Secure sites have https in the address or display a small padlock in the bottom right-hand corner of the screen.*

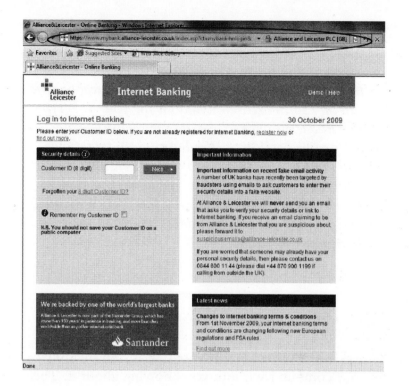

This is the log-on page for the Alliance and Leicester Bank. Notice that the address has the https at the beginning, that the address bar has changed to green and that there is a small padlock icon. All of these indicate that this site has extra security on it. Do not disclose any personal information unless the site has these showing.

SPYWARE/ADWARE

This is software that installs itself on your computer without you knowing about it. It can do this any time you are on the Internet. It can collect personal information that you fill in when online.

What to do about it:

- *You can download free software from the Internet that will check your computer for spyware, or you can buy software that will do it for you. This type of software is called spyware removal software.*
- *Keep your version of Windows up to date. Once you have bought Windows you are entitled to free updates from their website (www.microsoft.com). When you are logged onto the Internet, Windows will prompt you when updates are ready for your computer.*

16.3 Viruses and worms

Viruses and worms are software that install themselves on your computer without you knowing about it. This normally happens when you download something from the Internet or when you open an email. Like human viruses, a computer virus or worm will infect your computer causing all sorts of problems. Some are worse than others. Really bad ones will delete everything on your computer.

What to do about it:

- *Download only from reputable sites or secure sites as explained above.*
- *Do not open emails (especially email attachments) if you do not know who they are from.*

- *Delete any spam emails immediately and do not open them.*
- *Use anti-virus software. You can get free software from the Internet or you can buy it from companies such as McAfee or Norton.*
- *Keep your anti-virus software up to date as new viruses come out every day.*
- *Keep your version of Windows up to date as many updates contain fixes for well-known viruses.*

16.4 Hacking

Hacking is when someone gains unauthorized access to your computer. They can do this any time you are connected to the Internet. You will not even know that it is happening. Hackers do it for various reasons. Often it is just bored teenagers, but some hackers do it with the intention of getting your personal information.

What to do about it:

- *Install a firewall. This is software and hardware that examines information that is being passed to your computer while you are online. If it finds something it doesn't like, it will block it. If you are using Windows you will already have a firewall.*
- *Turn off the Internet. Only stay online (connected to the Internet) if you need to be. At other times, log yourself off. To do this:*

1 *Click on the 'Start' icon, and then 'Connect to'.*

2 *Click on 'All Connections'. You will be shown any connections that are currently being made between you and the outside world. You will see one with the word 'connected' next to it.*

3 *Right click any connection that is connected and select 'Disconnect'.*

16.5 Undesirable material

The unregulated nature of the Internet means that you can get access to plenty of undesirable material. Often you will click on a site that you think is perfectly innocent only to find that it contains undesirable content. This may be of particular concern if children have access to your computer.

What to do about it:

▶ *Use your common sense. If you don't like what you see, click on the cross immediately to close the website.*

▶ *Install filtering or blocking software. This special software allows you to block access to sites that contain undesirable content.*

▶ *Set the 'Content Advisor' or use the 'Parental controls' available in Windows 7. This is like the filtering/blocking software mentioned above but is already built-in to Windows. To set it:*

1 *Open 'Internet Explorer' if it is not open already, from the Start menu or Taskbar.*

2 *Select 'Tools' in the top right-hand corner.*

3 *Select 'Internet Options', which is at the bottom of the list.*

4 *Click on the 'Content' tab as shown. Notice that you can also access the Parental Controls from this window.*

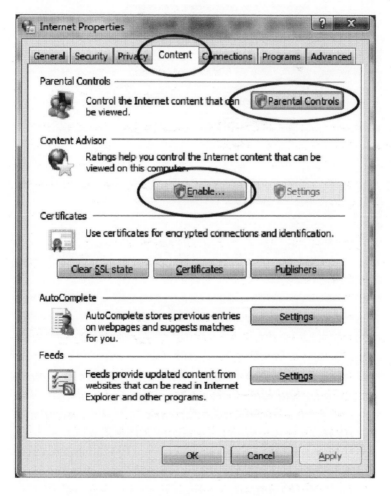

5 *Click on 'Enable'. The following screen is displayed.*

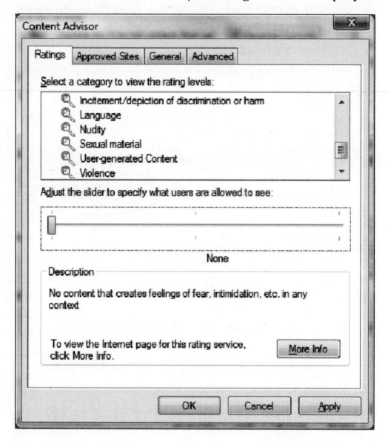

6 *It lists a number of categories of offensive content such as bad language, nudity, sex and violence. You can now select a rating for each of these categories by moving the slider to 'None', 'Limited' or 'Unrestricted'.*

7 *You can also set parental controls, which allow you to limit the amount of time someone has on the Internet or restrict access to certain sites. This will*

*only work if you have several users set up on the
computer and if one of them is an Administrator.
Click on the 'Parental Control' option and you will
see the following window:*

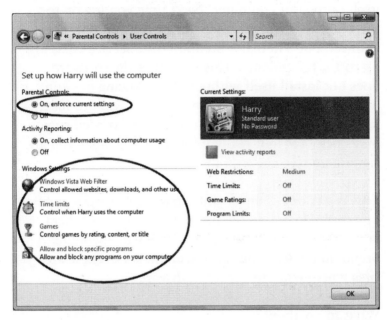

8 *You can click on the 'On, enforce current settings'
button and go through the options in the bottom
left-hand corner setting them up as you think
appropriate.*

Hints and tips

As there is so much undesirable content on the
Internet, these filters are not 100% effective. It
is recommended that you buy specialist filtering/
blocking software if you are particularly concerned
about it.

16.6 Premium diallers

A premium dialler is a piece of software that installs itself onto your computer. Next time you log on to the Internet it will not use your normal number to connect, but will dial a premium rate service charging up to £1.50 a minute. This is legal as the software does not install itself without you knowing it – you will see a message that asks you if you want to install it. However, the message is not clearly worded so you may click 'Yes' not really understanding what you are signing up to.

This is a tricky scam as you often see messages popping up when you are on the Internet, and most of them are fairly benign. You are most likely to encounter a premium dialler scam on download sites. These are sites where you can get free software.

What to do about it:

▶ *Read all messages carefully before clicking 'Yes' whenever you are on the Internet.*
▶ *Phone your telephone service provider and ask them to block all outgoing calls to premium rate numbers.*
▶ *Only use reputable sites.*

16.7 Unreliable sites

Many of the problems described in this chapter come from unreliable sites. But how do you spot a dodgy site? It is not always easy as even bad websites can be made to look good.

What to do about it:

- ▶ *Don't click on a link to a website that comes from an unsolicited email.*
- ▶ *Use only sites of well-known businesses or sites that are recommended.*
- ▶ *Avoid sites that offer free downloads, free movies, free music, free games or file-sharing.*
- ▶ *Ensure the site is secure – look for the https and the padlock symbol.*

16.8 Buying online

When you buy anything online there is always a danger that the goods will not be delivered, or that what is delivered, is not what you ordered.

What to do about it:

- ▶ *Buy only from trusted websites. This could be the websites of large companies or those that have been recommended by a friend.*

- *Keep copies of all receipts. All decent online stores will provide a screen where you can print a copy of your order. Most will also send an email to confirm the order.*
- *Check for a real address so that you can contact them if something goes wrong. It is preferable if they are located in the same country as you!*
- *Use your common sense. If a deal looks too good to be true – it probably isn't true.*
- *Have a separate credit/debit card that you use for online transactions and have only a small credit limit on it.*
- *Use secure payment services such as PayPal. These provide insurance against non-delivery.*

16.9 Passwords

Passwords usually in combination with a user name are required all over the place. Your computer itself will probably require a user name and password. Email sites, online auctions, chat rooms, etc. all require you to register with a user name and password.

Passwords are very important and keep you safe online. There are some rules that you should follow:

- *Never ever give your password to anyone else.*
- *Change your password regularly and don't use the same password twice.*

- *Don't choose something obvious like names, dates of birth, etc. Use combinations of letters, numbers and other characters, as they are harder to guess.*
- *Don't write passwords down anywhere.*

16.10 Don't have nightmares ...

Internet crime is increasing and you are never immune to threats even if you take all of the precautions listed in this chapter. However, if you take precautions, the chances of becoming a victim are small. Remember that millions of people now use the Internet regularly with no problems.

IMPORTANT THINGS TO REMEMBER FROM THIS CHAPTER

1 *There are some risks involved in using the Internet due to the ease in which people can get online and the lack of regulation.*

2 *Identity theft is when someone obtains personal details about you and uses these to their own advantage – usually to commit a fraud.*

3 *You should keep all of your personal details secure and never disclose them to anyone.*

4 *Malicious computer programs can install themselves on your computer when you are connected to the Internet.*

5 *You can protect against adware and spyware using special software, some of which is available for free.*

6 *Your computer and the data on it can be at risk from viruses. You can protect against these using anti-virus software.*

7 *Hackers are people that access your computer remotely while you are online. You can protect against these using a 'firewall'.*

8 *There is some nasty material on the Internet. You can filter a lot of it out using settings in Windows.*

9 *You should exercise the same caution online as you do in the real world. If something is too good to be true it probably isn't true.*

10 *Millions of people use the Internet every day and the majority do not experience any problems, but you do need to be aware of the risks.*

17

Getting photographs from a digital camera onto your PC

In this chapter you will learn
- *how to connect the camera to the computer*
- *how to copy images from the camera to the computer*
- *browsing and editing photographs*
- *printing photographs*

17.1 Introduction

When you take a photograph with a digital camera, the photo is stored on a card that is plugged into the camera. Eventually this card will get full of photographs and your camera will not let you take any more pictures. When this happens, you need to delete some of the photos. However, if you do this, those photographs become permanently deleted (i.e. they are gone forever).

What you need to do, therefore, is copy the photographs from the camera and store them on your computer. This process is sometimes referred to as uploading. Your computer's hard disk has a much larger storage capacity than your camera so you will be able to store thousands of photographs on your computer.

Also, once the photographs are on the computer you can do other things with them. The most common thing you might want to do is print them out. However, you can also edit them, perhaps adjusting the brightness or contrast of individual photographs.

17.2 Getting started

There are hundreds of different digital cameras available. When you buy a digital camera, you will be supplied with a CD that contains special software that is used to upload the photographs from the camera. Windows 7 is also has features built into it that allow you to upload and manage your photographs. It is up to you whether you use the specialist software or Windows 7. The specialist software may contain some additional features that you might find useful. The advantage of using Windows is that you can just plug your camera into your computer and no extra software needs to be installed. This chapter will use Windows 7.

17.3 Connecting the camera to the computer

First, you need to connect the camera to the computer. This is done using a lead that will have been provided when you bought the camera. One end of the lead plugs into the camera and the other end plugs into one of the USB ports.

1 *Connect your camera to your computer.*
2 *Switch on the camera.*

Most cameras have two settings. You should switch it to the setting that allows you to view the photographs you have taken, rather than the one that allows you to take photographs.

On some cameras, you have to press a button on the camera to tell it that it is connected to the computer. You should see a message in the bottom right-hand corner to indicate that the camera has been plugged in that reads: 'New hardware found'. You may also hear a noise when you plug in.

There is a possibility that the computer will not recognize that the camera has been plugged in. If this is the case, you will see a message saying that the camera can't be found. If this happens:

3 *Disconnect and then reconnect the camera, and make sure it is switched on. Check the LCD screen on the camera as it may be giving you instructions too. You should now see a window that looks like the one shown below. This window is displayed whenever you plug in any device that stores information.*

4 *You will see that there is an option to 'Import pictures and video' but at this stage we will look at the images first so click on 'Open folder to view files' as shown.*

Hints and tips

Digital cameras use up batteries quickly so don't leave your camera on unnecessarily. You can buy power adapters so that you can plug them into the mains. When your camera is plugged into your computer, it will usually take its power from the computer rather than the batteries.

17.4 Viewing the images

You are now able to view all of the images that are stored on your camera. The advantage of viewing them first is that you can delete any that you do not want to keep at this stage. You can also simply import them all and delete them later if you wish.

When you first view the folder it may be showing lots of files with names that are not that useful as shown in the example below:

Change your view

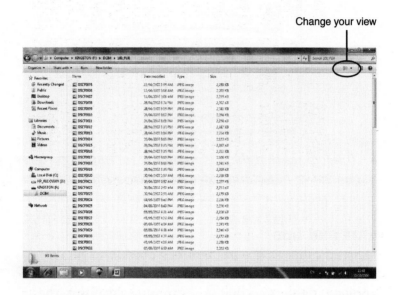

Note that the camera automatically names the files, e.g. DSCF0819. You can also see that the file types are jpeg, which is a common format for photographs.

To make it easier we can change the view so that it shows us a thumbnail image of the photographs.

▶ *Click on the 'Change your view' icon as shown in the image above and select 'Large icons'.*

There are various options that relate to how big the images are so you might like to experiment with these. You will now see the images rather than the file names as shown below:

You can now view each of your images. If you want to view any of them full screen, double click on the image. You will notice that some media player controls are displayed, so that you can view the photographs as a slideshow or simply click on the cross to go back to the thumbnail view. This is the Windows Photo Viewer. Note that there are some additional features in this software such as the ability to burn your photographs onto a CD or print them out. You can also delete photos from here.

To delete any image:

1 *Click on it and press the DELETE key.*

2 Click 'OK' to confirm. It is probably best to delete any images you don't want at this stage rather than uploading them and then deleting them later.

3 If you want to delete more than one image at a time, hold down the CTRL key and click on each image you want to delete.

4 When you have clicked on all the images you want to get rid of, press the DELETE key and 'OK' to confirm. This deletes the images permanently from your camera.

17.5 Uploading the photographs

You now need to tell it where to upload (save) the images. For now, you can upload them to the Pictures library, which is already set up for you. Chapter 19 provides more information on how to organize your work into libraries and folders.

1 Click on 'Organize' in the top left-hand corner.

2 Click on 'Select all'. You will see that all the images are selected as they go a darker colour.

3 Right click and select 'Copy'.

4 Click on 'Pictures' on the left-hand side.

5 Right click anywhere in the window that has just opened.

6 Click on 'Paste'. All of the images are now copied from your camera to your computer. Note that they are still on the camera as well.

7 Switch off the camera and disconnect it from the computer.

17.6 Deleting photographs from your camera

Once the photos have been uploaded successfully, you can safely delete them from the camera. All cameras have an option to delete individual photographs or all photographs in one go. This varies from camera to camera.

Another thing you might want to do from time to time is to create a separate copy of all of your photographs just in case they accidentally get lost or deleted from your computer. There is more information on this in Chapter 20.

17.7 Editing photographs

To make changes to your photographs, for example, adjusting the brightness or contrast, you will need to use specialized software. This will have been supplied on a CD or DVD when you bought the camera. You can also buy additional photo editing software such as Adobe PhotoShop, which allows you to manipulate your images in even more creative ways.

17.8 Printing photographs

You can print out your photographs either from the camera software or from the Windows Photo Viewer.

Hints and tips

Some cameras come with a printer and all you have to do is plug your camera straight into the printer.

To print from the camera software:

1 *Select the photograph.*
2 *Select 'File' and the 'Print' from the Menu bar, or click the 'Print' icon in the toolbar.*

To print from Windows Photo Viewer:

▶ *Click on the photograph you want to print and select 'Print' from the Command bar. You can also right click on a picture and select 'Print' from the menu.*

Modern printing techniques mean that you will get a good quality image even if printing on standard A4 photocopier paper. Alternatively, you can pay more for photo quality paper.

Hints and tips

Printed photographs often fade quite quickly on standard paper, so if you want the photograph to last, photo quality paper is recommended.

IMPORTANT THINGS TO REMEMBER FROM THIS CHAPTER

1 *Photographs taken with a digital camera are stored on a card in it. You can upload the images onto your computer.*

2 *Your camera will have software and a lead to connect it to the computer. You can use this special software or Windows 7 own routines.*

3 *When you connect you camera to the computer, Windows will spot that it has been plugged in and will display the photographs on the screen.*

4 *One of the big advantages of digital cameras is that you can take as many shots as you like and delete the dodgy ones later.*

5 *You can view the images either as thumbnails where you can see several on the screen, or on whole screen in a slideshow.*

6 *You can upload photographs into a suitable location on the computer. You might want to delete some individual photographs.*

7 *You can delete photographs off the camera once you have a safe copy on the computer. This frees up the camera's card so you can take new shots.*

8 *You can do some basic editing, such as rotating images, in Windows.*

9 *You can use specialized software to edit the images in various ways. For example, you might want to adjust the brightness or contrast.*

10 *You can also print out your images either into ordinary paper or onto special photography paper, which will give a better finish and will last longer.*

18

Scanning photographs into your computer

In this chapter you will learn
- *how to use a scanner*
- *how to scan photographs*
- *how to adjust photographs*
- *how to save photographs on the computer*
- *how to adjust the quality (resolution) of the image*
- *how to use 'one-touch' scanning*

18.1 Introduction

A flatbed scanner turns a paper-based image into a digital one on the computer. There are many situations where you might want to scan an image. For example, if you find an image in a book and would like to use it on the computer, or as in this case, if you have old photographs that you would like to store on the computer. You can scan anything you like – it does not have to be an image. The process is exactly the same.

The advantage of scanning an image is that although your photographs may fade over time, or become damaged, a digital image is relatively secure on your computer.

This chapter assumes that you have a scanner and that it is ready to use with the computer. If you have just bought a new scanner and have not plugged it in yet, see Chapter 5 for instructions on how to install it. Alternatively, if you simply plug it in, Windows 7 will attempt to load the software automatically from the Internet.

18.2 Getting started

When you buy a scanner, it will come with its own software. You can either choose to use this specialized software or you can use one of the Windows Fax and Scan utility. Both will work in very similar ways. In this chapter, the latter will be used.

1 *Check that your scanner is plugged in, switched on and connected to your computer.*
2 *Lift the lid of the scanner.*
3 *Place the photograph face down on the top right-hand corner of the glass plate.*
4 *Close the lid.*
5 *Open the scanner software by clicking to the Start menu, selecting 'All programs' and then 'Windows Fax and Scan'. Some scanners have a 'one-touch'*

scanning option. This means that there is a button on the scanner, which will do this bit for you. Check if your scanner has this. There are more details on this at the end of this chapter.

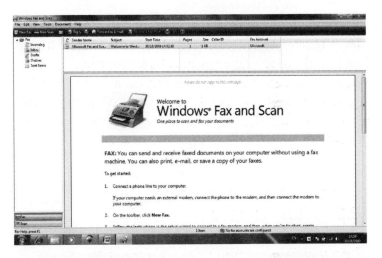

Hints and tips

Scanners use light reflection so it is important that the lid is closed, otherwise you will get lots of black on your images.

18.3 Scanning an image

1 *Click on 'New Scan' and the New Scan window is displayed (see page 240).*
2 *Click on 'Preview'. After a few seconds your scanner will begin to scan and the image will be displayed in the window. The purpose of the*

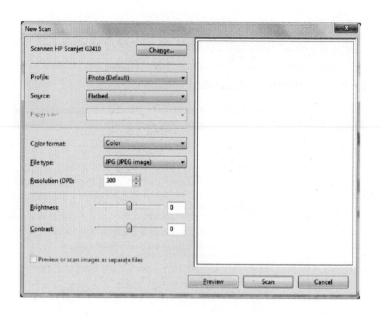

*preview is to show you what the image will look
like when it is saved. If there is anything wrong
with it, you need to adjust it now.*

3 *In the example below, the photograph is not on
straight, so it needs scanning again. You would need
to lift the lid and straighten the photograph on the
glass, and then click 'New Scan' again.*

4 *There are editing options that you might want to
experiment with. For example, it is possible to
adjust the brightness or the colour contrast of the
photograph at this point by moving the sliders. As
you adjust the settings, the preview will change to
show you the effect of the adjustments.*

In most cases, none of these adjustments will be
necessary and you can save the image straight away.

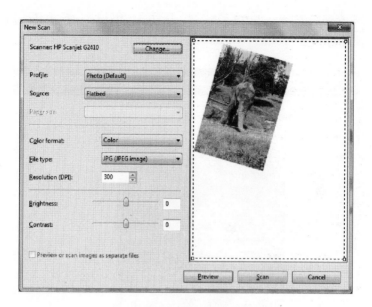

Notice that you can change the "resolution" here too. There is more on this in section 18.5.

18.4 Saving the image

1 *To accept the image that you can see in the preview, click on 'Scan'. It will then scan the image again with the final settings, which you may or may not*

have changed. The image is then displayed as shown below:

2 *Click on 'Save as'. The following window is displayed. Notice that the file type is set to 'jpeg', which is a standard format for photographs. Windows automatically puts scanned images into a folder called 'Scanned Documents' but you can put the image wherever you want it.*

3 *Click on the little arrow next to where it reads 'Scanned Documents' as shown. Form here you can move around the libraries and folders on the computer. For example, you may want to put this image in the Pictures library.*

4 *After you have chosen which folder you want to put it in, give the file any file name you like. As when*

*saving any files, it is best to give it a meaningful
name that you can recognize later on. In this case
the file is called: Elephant – Bristol Zoo 2009.*

5 *You can now continue by putting the next
photograph on the scanner and so on.*

Hints and tips

You might find it helpful to date the file name
of your photographs for future reference.
Some scanning software creates new folders
automatically with the current date on them.

There are more details in Chapter 19 about managing
your files and folders. Don't worry too much if you
have put them in the wrong folder as you can always
move them later on.

18.5 Problems with file size and resolution

Every time a file is saved on your computer, it takes up some space on the hard disk where all files are stored. Photographs are stored in files and take up a lot of space. If you also use a digital camera, you will have come across this problem already, in that you can store only a limited number of photographs on the camera at any one time.

This is not necessarily a problem if you have a fairly new computer with a decent amount of hard disk space (e.g. anything over 200 GB). However, if you plan to store thousands of photographs, you might run out of space. Another problem is that if you want to send photographs to other people (perhaps as email attachments), then large files take much longer to send.

To give you an idea, a typical good quality scanned photograph will take up 100 times more space than a typical Word document.

In Chapter 2, the idea of resolution was introduced. On a digital camera, you can choose between high resolution and low resolution (and often a few other settings in-between). High resolution images are better quality but take up much more space on your camera and on your computer.

When you scan an image, you can set the resolution to whatever you like ranging from 75dpi (dots per inch) to several thousand; 90dpi is sufficient for most photographs even though your scanner software will probably be set to 200–300dpi. Windows Fax and Scan is set to 300dpi.

Hints and tips

dpi is a measure of the quality of an image. It stands for dots per inch.

18.6 One-touch scanning

Many modern scanners now have a one-touch scanning facility. This means that there will be a button on the scanner, which when pressed will automatically open the scanner software and scan the image for you. This will work to the standard settings.

The disadvantage is that you have less control over the settings, but if you are happy with the standard settings (which are fine in most cases), then this option will save you some time.

IMPORTANT THINGS TO REMEMBER FROM THIS CHAPTER

1 A flatbed scanner is a device a bit like a photocopier that turns a paper-based image or document into a computerized image.

2 A common use of a scanner is to make a digital copy of old photographs that were taken using traditional cameras with film.

3 Windows has its own built-in software, which will work with most scanners.

4 When you scan, you can do a preview first to check that it is scanning correctly.

5 There are various options for editing the image, for example, adjusting the brightness as the scan is completed.

6 After you have scanned the image it is saved in a file, much the same a digital photograph.

7 You could store your scanned images in the Pictures library. You might want to create separate folders within this library.

8 *A scanned image can take up a lot of room on your hard disk. How much it takes up comes down to the resolution of the image.*

9 *The higher the resolution the clearer the image will be but the more space the image will take up on the computer.*

10 *Some scanners have a one-touch feature which means that all you have to do is press the button on the scanner and it will do everything for you.*

19

Keeping track of photographs and other files

In this chapter you will learn
- *where photographs are stored on the computer*
- *how to create folders to store photographs in*
- *how to move photographs into new folders*
- *how to view several photographs at the same time using thumbnails*
- *how to rename photographs*
- *how to delete photographs*

19.1 Introduction

You may already have lots of files on your computer. There are many different types of files all of which contain different information. For example, a file might be a Word document, a photograph, a music track or a movie.

In Chapter 4 you were introduced to Windows Explorer and the four libraries that are already set up on your computer called Documents, Music, Pictures and Videos. You don't have to use these libraries but it makes sense to do so. For example, you can keep your photographs in the Pictures library. Most software is set up so that when you save your work, it will automatically go to the right library. For example, Word documents get saved into the Documents library. The problem is that after a while you could have hundreds of documents in this folder, which makes it difficult to keep track of them all.

This chapter will show you how to use the Windows Explorer feature in Windows 7 to manage all of your files.

19.2 Getting started

We will use some of the files that we have created throughout this book so far as examples. To start with, there are three levels: libraries, folders and files. A library can contain many folders and a folder can contain many files (or further folders).

You probably already have several photographs in the Pictures library, which we are going to rename and then move into a new folder that will be created for them.

1 *Click on the 'Start' icon and select 'Pictures'. This opens the library in Windows Explorer. Notice that you can also open the Music and Documents* *libraries directly from here too. Once Explorer is open you can move around to any library or folder on your computer but it is easier to start here to try and understand the structure.*

2 *A window will open showing the contents of the Pictures library.*

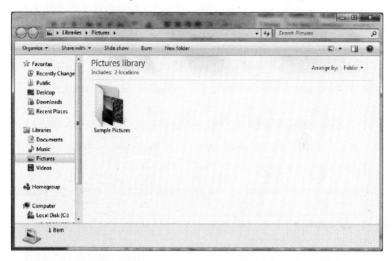

3 *You are now inside a library. There can be two things inside a library – either folders or files. Within a folder there can be either more folders and or files. This can get confusing. If you get lost at any time, click on the 'Back' button in exactly the same way as when using the Internet. This will take you back to the folder before.*

It might help to think of it like a family tree. At the top of the tree is Pictures and then everything else branches off from that. In this example above, there is one folder called 'Sample pictures'. You can tell it is a folder because it has a yellow folder icon.

Notice on the left-hand side that you can also move to the Documents, Video or Music libraries, which in turn will contain folders and files.

19.3 Using the thumbnail view

The thumbnail view is really useful and is used in all sorts of circumstances on a computer. It means that several small images are displayed on the same screen allowing you to see a small (thumbnail) version of the image.

1 *Double click on the 'Sample Pictures' folder. The folder will open and in it you will see several files. In this case they are photographs.*

2 *In the example above, there are only a few images in the folder so you can see them all on the one screen. If there were more, you might have to scroll down in the window in order to see them all.*
3 *To see a larger version of an image, double click on the thumbnail image.*

4 *When you have viewed the image, click on the cross in the top right-hand corner of this window and you are taken back to the Pictures library. You will notice that this is exactly the same process as when you were viewing scanned photographs.*

19.4 Renaming a file

All information is stored in files. Whether you are saving a letter, poster or photograph, they are all stored in files. It is often useful to rename the files so that the file name makes more sense.

The example below shows several images taken with a digital camera that have been uploaded. At the moment they are in the Pictures library. Most digital cameras automatically give each photograph a file name, and this file name is usually something pretty useless like PIC0000111. To rename a file, you can view the thumbnail of it and then rename it with a name that is appropriate to the image.

In the example below, a new file has been added from the digital camera. The camera has called it DSCF0826.

To rename the file:

1 *Right click on the image.*
2 *Select 'Rename' from the list.*
3 *You can now type in a sensible name, for example: Pisa*

It is important that you type the .jpg bit as this is what tells the computer that it is a photograph.

If you had lots of files, perhaps if you have just downloaded lots from your digital camera, you could have a session on the computer where you just work your way through renaming all the files.

19.5 Creating new folders

Another useful way of keeping track of your files is to create separate folders. In this case we are going to create a folder inside the Pictures library for different sets of photos.

For example, you might have a folder called Holiday Pictures, one called Family Pictures, etc., or you might create a folder using the date as a name as has been done in the case above. You can have folders within folders so you might set up further folders within the Holiday Pictures folder called, for example, Summer 2009, Summer 2010 etc.

Hints and tips

Some software for digital cameras and scanners will create these folders for you automatically, whether you want them or not!

The problem with using dates for folder names is that it is unlikely that you will remember when the photos were taken, so after a while the folder name becomes pretty useless. If your software does create folders for you using dates, then rename them in exactly the same way as you rename a file, using the right click and Rename option.

To create a new folder:

1 *Right click anywhere where there is white space in the folder. This will display a menu.*

Hints and tips

The right click options vary depending on where you right click. To create a new folder, you must right click somewhere in the folder, but not on a file.

2 *Select 'New' and then select 'Folder'.*
3 *A new folder is created within the current folder called 'New Folder'.*

4 *Type in a new name for this folder, for example:*
Italy Trip 2009.

You now have a folder that you can use to put in all of
the photographs from this particular trip. The folder
name is useful as it will help you to remember what is
in the folder at a later date.

19.6 Moving files into folders

It would make sense to create any new folders before
you start downloading images. Then you can tell the
computer to put the images straight into your new folder.

It is also possible to move files around between folders
and to have several copies of the same file in different
folders.

To move a file:

1 *Right click on the file that you want to move. In this example, we will move the Pisa photograph into the Italy Trip 2009 folder.*

2 *Select 'Cut' from the list.*

3 *Double click on the Italy trip folder. This will now open this folder, which at the moment will not have anything it.*

4 *Right click in the white space at the bottom of the window.*

5 *Right click, and select 'Paste'. The photograph is then moved from the Pictures library into the Italy trip folder. You can repeat this process for each photograph. If you want to move several files at the same time:*

6 *Hold down the CTRL key and then click on each files that you want to copy.*

7 *Release the CTRL key and right click.*

8 *Now carry out the cut and paste as before.*

It is possible to view the contents of your folders in different ways. The standard view is called 'Large icons' where each of your files or folders is shown as an icon.

To switch between these different views:

▶ *Select 'View' from the menus and click on 'List' or 'Small icons' depending on which you prefer.*

You might want to experiment with the other views while you are here.

19.7 Deleting a file

If you ever want to delete a file, you can do this from here. Deleting a file will remove it from the library or folder that it is in and put it into the Recycle bin. The file is not permanently deleted. The idea of this is that if you do delete a file by accident, you can go to the Recycle Bin, which you can find on the desktop, and recover the file you deleted.

You might choose to delete files if you don't want to keep them (e.g. a particularly embarrassing photo), or if you already have the file somewhere else, or if you start to run out of space on your computer.

To delete a file:

1 *Right click on the file you want to delete.*
2 *Click 'Delete'.*
3 *Click 'OK' when it asks if you are sure.*

To recover a file you have deleted:

4 *Double click on the Recycle Bin from your desktop.*
5 *All deleted files will be listed in alphabetical order. Find the file you want to open and double-click on it.*

Hints and tips

To delete a file permanently, you also need to delete it from the Recycle Bin. You should not rely on always being able to find deleted files in the Recycle Bin as it can only store a certain number of files and eventually it will get full. When this happens it will permanently delete the files that have been in there the longest.

19.8 Understanding the folder structure

Getting to grips with the folder structure is complicated. There are already hundreds of folders on your computer used to store all of the files for the software that you are running. Every time you install new software, a new batch of folders will be created. Folders within folders within folders ...

You do have to be careful when exploring your folders that you don't move anything or delete it unless you are absolutely sure what it is. This could stop your computer from working properly. As a general rule, you should not touch anything in the Program Files or Windows folders, and never delete a System file. By default, those files and folders that the computer needs to function properly are hidden, and they are best kept so that they cannot be moved or deleted by accident.

The best approach is to only use the Pictures library for your pictures, the Music library for your music and the Documents library for your other work, e.g. Word documents. As you use the computer more you can start to create folders and sub-folders within each folder. You can create as many sub-folders as you like. You will have to remember what you have put into all these sub-folders so give them sensible names.

To understand the overall structure of your folders you need to look in the left-hand side of the window.

This shows the family tree idea mentioned before. At the top is the Desktop, then the various folders branch off from this. One of the folders within it is the Pictures folder and within that there is a further sub-folder called Russia trip used in the example.

You can see how quickly the folder structure grows when you are using your computer. For new users of computers, this is often one of the hardest things to understand, so don't worry if you haven't quite got it yet. Every time you save a file of any sort, you will see the folder structure again, which is another chance to get to grips with it!

19.9 Working with windows

You notice that it is very easy to end up with lots of different windows open. For example, to move a file from one folder to another requires you to have two windows open at the same time. At the same time, you may have some software programs open and maybe you are on the Internet as well.

Windows 7 contains some handy features to help you manage all of these open windows. You have seen some of these already in Chapter 4.

For a thumbnail view of what is open, hold the mouse of each icon in the Taskbar at the bottom of the screen. For example, the first image below shows what you would see if you held the mouse over the Internet Explorer icon. The main screen still shows what you were working on last. In this case it is the Pictures library open in Windows Explorer. In this example, the Internet open in the background and it is on the Tiscali home page. If there were several Internet pages open they would be shown as thumbnails here.

1 *To switch to this window simply click on it.*

2 *To close this window you will see a small red cross in the top right-hand corner of the thumbnail. As an alternative you can right click and select 'Close'.*

Another useful feature is that if you want to look at two windows at the same time you can 'snap' them so that they both take up exactly half the screen.

1 *To do this you need to left click and hold in the dark blue bar at the top of the first window. Then move it to the right-hand side of the screen and let go of the mouse button. It will snap into place taking up exactly half the screen.*

2 *Do the same with the second window but this time move it to the left. You can now look at both windows at the same time. You can resize these windows at any time by clicking and holding and then moving anywhere on the frame of the window that you want to re-size. Remember that you can always use the 'Maximize' and 'Restore' icons in the very top right-hand corner of each window.*

A final feature is the ability to close all of your open windows in one go so that you just leave the one you want open. To do this:

1 *Left click and hold on the dark blue bar at the top of the window that you want to leave open.*
2 *Now shake the mouse.*

You will see that all open windows become minimized leaving this window open. These are available from the Taskbar in the usual way if you want to open them again.

IMPORTANT THINGS TO REMEMBER FROM THIS CHAPTER

1 *Everything that is stored in your computer is stored in a file. A file is stored within a folder, which in turn is stored within a library.*

2 *There are four main libraries which are set up to store documents, pictures, music and videos.*

3 *To view the contents of libraries and folders you use Windows Explorer.*

4 *You can rename your files to give them more useful names.*

5 *You can create new folders within the libraries or new folders within a folder. Think of it like a giant filing cabinet.*

6 *You can move files around within folders so that you know where everything is and delete files that you no longer need at any time.*

7 *When you delete a file, it is moved to the Recycle Bin and can be recovered from there if needed.*

8 *Windows 7 has some useful features to make it easier to work with Windows Explorer.*

9 *Windows will show you a thumbnail view of all the windows you have open at any one time making it easier to move between windows.*

10 *You can also minimize windows quickly by shaking the one you want left open or compare two windows by snapping them into place on the screen.*

20

Copying files onto CD,
DVD and memory stick

In this chapter you will learn
- *what a backup is and why you need to do it*
- *how to make a copy of your work*
- *how to copy information onto DVD, CD and memory stick*

20.1 Introduction

There are several reasons why you might want to create a copy of your work. The main reason is to create a backup so that if anything goes wrong on your computer, you still have the files stored elsewhere.

You might also want to copy files onto a portable device such as a CD, DVD or memory stick so that you can move files from one computer to another, or if you want to give someone else a copy of something that you have done on your computer.

If you download music, video or software from the Internet, you could create a copy on a CD or DVD so that you can keep a safe copy of it.

20.2 Creating a backup

A backup is a complete separate version of files or folders that is stored onto a separate device away from the computer. The purpose of a backup is so that if you lose any of the files on your computer for whatever reason, you still have a safe copy somewhere that you can then put back onto your computer.

Files can get deleted by accident, or destroyed by a virus, or your computer could crash (stop working because of a software problem) and destroy files. The first one on this list is actually the most likely. You can create a backup as often as you like. You should probably aim to do one at least once a month. You do not need to back up everything on your computer, just your data files, as you should have the original disks for software and the Windows operating system, and can restore them from these.

In Chapter 19, you looked at how you can create new folders. Usually these would be new folders inside libraries or sub-folders within folders. If you do this it means most of your work will be stored somewhere in the Documents, Pictures, Music or Video folders. Doing it this way makes it easier to know which files and folders to back up as you can simply back up everything that is contained within these folders.

There are different ways of creating a backup, but the most common is to back up onto CD or DVD. In Chapter 2 we looked at buying either a DVD or CD writer for this purpose – this is the tray that opens up into which you place the CD or DVD.

Hints and tips

Although DVDs are associated with films, they can actually be used for storing any type of information and can store much more than a CD.

This chapter assumes that you have either one of these. Most computers will have one or the other, not usually both. The process for creating a backup is the same regardless. You will also need to have some CDs or DVDs onto which to create the backup. These must be CD-R, CD-RW, DVD-R or DVD-RW.

▶ *CD-R and DVD-R disks can have files copied onto them once. You can put only one set of files on them but you can copy the files back from the CD at any time.*
▶ *CD-RW and DVD-RW disks can be used over and over again. This means that you can use the same CD or DVD each time you back up.*

Hints and tips

CD-R and DVD-R disks are cheaper to buy than the RW versions and are ideal for backups.

20.3 Selecting the files or folders to backup

In this example, parts of the Documents library will be backed up:

1 *Open the CD/DVD tray by pressing the button located on the tower or desktop next to the tray itself.*
2 *Insert a blank CD or DVD into the drive, label up.*
3 *Close the CD/DVD tray.*

Your computer may prompt you with questions about what you want to do with the CD or DVD that you have just inserted. The messages are different depending on what type of CD or DVD you are using. You can either select one of the options or just close the window ignoring the message.

4 *Click on the 'Start' menu and select 'Documents'.*
5 *You can now select which folders and files you want to back up.*

To select all the folders and files within Documents:

6 *Click and hold, and drag the mouse pointer across all of the folders, or press CTRL and A at the same time. The folders and files will be shown as selected as they go a dark blue colour.*

To select specific files and folders:

7 *Click on the file or folder that you want. If you want more than one, use CTRL and click at the same time.*

This allows you to select several files or folders one at a time. In this case, the whole of the Documents library will be backed up.

8 *Press CTRL and A so that all files and folders are selected.*

9 *Right click on any of the selected folders or files and select 'Copy'.*

10 *The folder structure showing all of the folders on the whole computer will now be displayed on the left-hand side.*

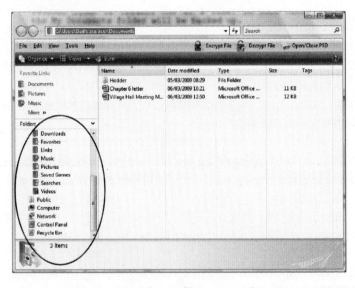

You want to copy these files onto the CD or DVD. To get to this you need to click on Computer in the list as shown. You may need to scroll down in this list to find it. You then need to find the CD or DVD drive in the main window. It will be called the CD or DVD Drive (depending on which one is on your

computer), and will have a letter after it in brackets, for example (D:).

11 *Select the CD or DVD Drive as shown:*

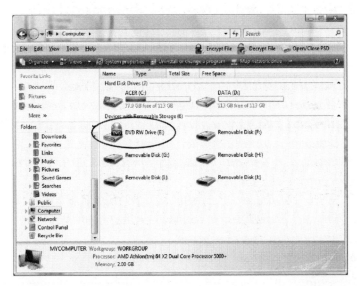

12 *This will take you to a new window, which displays the contents of the CD or DVD. As you have just put a new one in, there will be nothing on it and the window will be empty as shown.*

20.4 Pasting onto the CD or DVD

The next stage is to paste the files:

1 *You will be prompted to put a title on your CD/DVD if you want to, or it will use the date if you don't.*

The title is useful later as it will be displayed when you view the CD. If the title includes the date, this will also help to identify the backup. Click 'Next'.

2 *Right click anywhere in the white space of this window and select 'Paste'. This will paste all of the files/folders that you selected previously. On some systems, you might get some messages about 'stream loss'. If you do, just click on 'Yes'.*

3 *The backup will now begin. Depending on how many files and folders you have, this could take anywhere between a minute and ten minutes. When it has finished, it will automatically open the CD/DVD tray.*

4 *Remove the CD/DVD.*

5 *Write on the front of the disk so that you know what it is and put it somewhere safe, preferably away from the computer.*

6 *Click on 'Finish' on the wizard.*

Hints and tips

You can buy special pens for writing onto the CD surface. Don't use stickers as these may come off in the drive.

20.5 Running out of space on the CD/DVD

CDs and DVDs have room for only a certain number of files and folders. To give you an idea, a medium resolution (quality) photograph taken on a digital camera takes up about 1 megabyte (1MB). A music track takes up about 5MB. Most CDs have about 750MB on them, which means that you could store

750 photographs or 150 music tracks on one CD. DVDs can store roughly 10 times as many.

If you do run out of room on a CD or DVD, you will get an error message telling you that the disk is full. If this is the case, you will have to go back and select fewer files and folders, and try again.

20.6 Copying music and video files

If you are creating a copy of a music or video file to give to someone else, or perhaps to use on a different computer, the process is exactly the same as described for making a backup.

20.7 Copying files to a memory stick

Memory sticks are also known as memory keys, Flash drives or USB storage devices. They plug into a USB port and can be used for storing files and folders. They are not usually used for backup purposes, but only when files need transferring between computers.

They are useful devices to have if you ever need to move files between computers. For example: you might do an evening class and want to use files on your home computer and then take them into class; you might have more than one computer in your house and want to move files between computers.

The process of saving folders and files onto the memory stick is almost exactly the same as using a CD or DVD as described previously:

1 *Plug the memory stick into one of the USB ports. You should get a message telling you that new hardware has been detected and that it is ready to use.*
2 *Open the 'Documents' folder.*
3 *Select the files or folders that you want to copy.*
4 *Right click on any of the selected files/folders and select 'Copy'.*
5 *Click on Computer as before.*
6 *Select 'Removable disk' and a new window is opened which shows the contents of your memory stick. If you have not used it before, it will be empty. There may be more than one removable disk being displayed with different letters attached to them. If you are not sure which one it is, double click on each of them. If you have got the wrong one you will get a message asking you to insert the removable disk. You will know it's the right one when a new window opens.*
7 *Now right click in the white space in this window and select 'Paste'.*

The files/folders are now written onto the memory stick and you can close down all of the open windows.

20.8 Safe removal of the memory stick

You can now just unplug the memory stick, but it is safer to tell Windows 7 that you are doing it. You should always follow this routine when unplugging any device attached to a USB port.

In the bottom right-hand corner of the screen, on the Taskbar there are a number of small icons.

1 *Click on the icon with a small green tick as shown.*

2 *It will show the label 'Safely Remove Hardware'. If you cannot see this icon, click on the small upward arrow to the left of the icons and a small menu will be displayed, which will show the icon.*
3 *A small menu will be displayed listing all of the devices plugged into USB ports. Click on the one that reads 'Eject USB disk'.*
4 *You can now safely remove the memory stick from the USB port.*

IMPORTANT THINGS TO REMEMBER FROM THIS CHAPTER

1 *A back-up is a copy of the important files on your computer that you store away from the computer in case you ever need them.*

2 *If you have kept all the original CDs or DVDs that were supplied with your software then you already have a back-up of these. You need to back up the files that you have created, e.g. documents, photographs etc.*

3 *The most common way of doing a back up is to copy important files onto a CD or DVD.*

4 *Your computer may have a CD or DVD drive. The DVD drive will handle DVDs and CDs.*

5 *If you have used the libraries correctly then every file you have created should be stored in one of them, so all you need to do is back up the libraries.*

6 *To back up, copy all of the files onto the CD/ DVD, then store it somewhere safe away from the computer.*

7 *A DVD will store approximately ten times more information than a CD.*

8 *If you don't have a DVD drive you may need to use several CDs to make sure that you have a copy of everything.*

9 *You can also use memory sticks to back files up although they are really designed for transferring information between computers.*

10 *If you do use a memory stick you should ensure that you 'eject' it properly or you could lose the files that you have stored on it.*

21

Making cards for all occasions

In this chapter you will learn
- *how to use Microsoft Publisher*
- *about different types of publication*
- *how to use the wizard to create an invitation card*
- *how to make changes to the invitation card*
- *how to save a print the invitation card*

21.1 Introduction

Microsoft Publisher is what is called desktop publishing software (DTP). It works in a similar way to Microsoft Word in that you can mix text and images together to make a publication. The big difference with Publisher is that it contains templates for hundreds of different types of publication including invitations, posters, leaflets and even websites.

One other thing to note about Publisher is that the options across the top of the screen are displayed slightly differently to Word. In Word (and all other Microsoft Office programs) you have the Microsoft office button, Quick Access Toolbar and then the Tabs that contain various options. In Publisher, you don't get all of this. Instead there are menu options. In fact this makes very little difference – it just looks different.

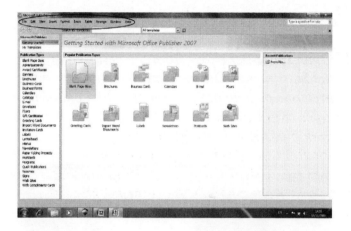

There are two main ways of using Publisher:

▶ *Using Publications types – this leads you through a set of screens asking you what publication you want and how you want it to look (this chapter looks at this method).*
▶ *Blank pages – this is where you start with a blank screen (like you do in Word) and you have to create the layout and put all the text and images in from scratch.*

You can choose which of these methods you want to use each time you create a new publication. Over the next three chapters, you will be shown both methods.

21.2 Getting started

1 *Open Publisher either from the desktop, or from the Start menu. The first screen as shown on the previous page will offer you all of the publication types (e.g. brochures, business cards, etc.) and the option of using blank pages.*

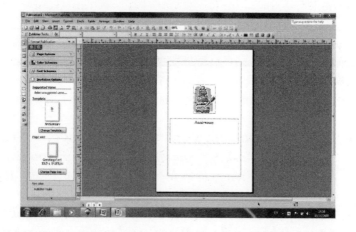

2 *If you look down the left-hand side you will see a full list of the publication types available. In this case you will be creating an invitation card although the principles explained here are the same for any type of card.*
3 *Select 'Invitation cards' from the list.*

4 *A further list is then displayed of all of the different invitation cards that are available. You will need to scroll down to see the whole list.*

5 *Scroll down until you find the section on 'Celebration'.*

6 *In the main window you will see lots of thumbnail views of different layouts that are available. You can scroll through these to find one that you think is appropriate. For this example, double click on 'Anniversary'. A basic layout is then created for your card.*

Your invitation is displayed in the main window and all of the options for changing it are shown in the pane on the left-hand side. Note that this is a four-page document. You can tell that by looking in the bottom left-hand corner as shown in the next diagram. Here you can see that it is a four-page document and we are looking at page 1.

These four pages are the front of the card, the inside pages and back of the card. When you print it out, this will become clearer.

There are lots of changes that you could make to this invitation but in this instance we are going to keep it simple. You will notice that an image has already been put onto the card and the heading 'Anniversary'.

1 *To add a verse, click on 'Invitation options' on the left-hand side and click on 'Select a suggested Verse'. Because we are using the invitation wizard, it knows that you might want to add in a particular phrase, so it has come up with some for you:*

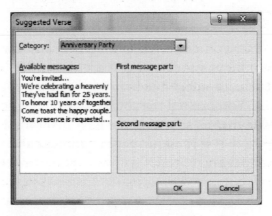

2 *If you click on each of the available messages, it will show you the message it will put on the front and on the inside of your publication.*

3 *For this example, click the last option and click 'OK'. This text will now be displayed on the inside or the card.*

4 *To view the inside of the card, click on the number 2 as shown in step 4 earlier. Notice that the pages you are looking at are highlighted in orange.*

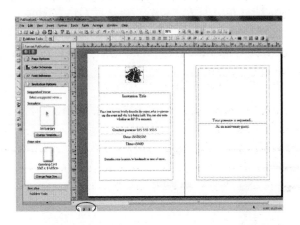

The main parts of the card are now complete but you will need to add more text and you may want to make changes to the standard publication.

21.3 Completing the card

You can now make changes to the invitation. You need to add some details to the inside of the invitation:

1 *Click on '2' where shown above. This will show you the inside of the invitation (which are actually pages 2 and 3).*

2 *Put in the details for your party. To change a piece of text, click on it. This will highlight it in black and you can type your own text. For example:*

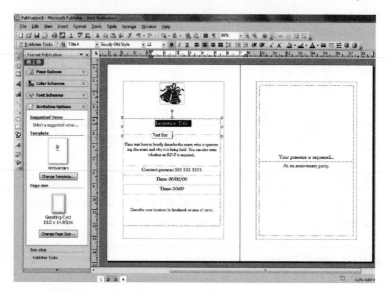

3 *Click on where it reads 'Invitation Title' and change this to 'Wedding Anniversary'.*

4 *Go through and change the other text to customize the details to your party.*

Hints and tips

Typing in new text is just the same as when you type text into Microsoft Word. Just click where you want to type – and type!

You could go on to make further changes if you wanted to, adding more text or more images, but for this example, the invitation is now finished.

21.4 Saving your work

By now, you might have been prompted to save your work. Publisher has a habit of reminding you every ten minutes or so that you have not saved your work yet. You should save about every ten minutes to be on the safe side.

If you are prompted to save your work, then do so when prompted. Or:

1 *Click on 'File' in the top left-hand corner of the screen and select 'Save' or on the 'Save' icon.*
2 *The file will be saved into the Documents folder unless you tell it otherwise. Type in a suitable file name, for example 'Wedding anniversary invitation' and click 'Save'.*

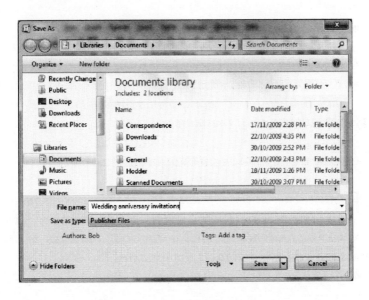

21.5 Printing your work

Printing from Publisher is pretty much the same as printing from any other software although you may have to put the publication together at the end. For example, when you type a letter, it prints onto A4 paper and you just fold it and send it. When printing an invitation like this, it will actually print out two sheets of A4 and you will have to put them together and fold them to create the card.

Hints and tips

It is recommended that you print out the invitation first as this bit is easier to understand with one in front of you.

You have two options:

▶ *Print out the invitation onto two sheets and then stick the two sheets back to back and fold in half to create the card.*
▶ *Print out the first sheet and then re-feed the paper into the printer so that it prints the second sheet on the other side of the same sheet of A4.*

To print the invitation on two sheets of paper:

1 *Click 'File' in the top left-hand corner and 'Print' and select 'OK'. In this example, two sheets of A4 will be printed. The first is the front and back of the card and the second is the inside of the card.*
2 *Now stick the two sheets back to back.*

To print the invitation on one sheet of paper:

1 *Click 'File' and 'Print'. The print options are now shown.*

2 *Rather than print both pages at the same time, click on 'Pages' as shown and type 1 in boxes. This just prints page 1.*

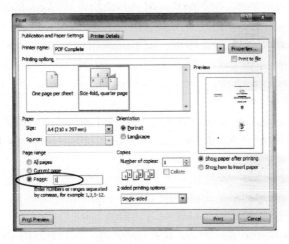

3 *When that has printed, take the printout and re-feed it into your printer so that you can print page 2 on the blank side.*

4 *Click 'Print' again and this time type 2 in the 'Pages' box. This will print page 2 only.*

5 *When you have finished, click on the cross to close Publisher.*

Hints and tips

All printers are different so there is no rule of thumb about which way to put in the paper to get it to print the right way round on the other side of the paper. It's a case of trial and error until you get it right.

IMPORTANT THINGS TO REMEMBER FROM THIS CHAPTER

1 *Microsoft Publisher is designed to create publications of different kinds. It can be used to create anything from an invitation to a web site.*

2 *Publisher has a range of publication types to choose from and uses templates, which are an efficient way of creating publications.*

3 *Publications may go across several pages and Publisher makes it easy to flick between pages.*

4 *Publisher uses frames. You must add the right type of frame and then put the content into the frame.*

5 *It is possible to use the 'wizard', which will guide you through the process step by step.*

6 *The wizard selects the right type of frame and locates them on the page into a suitable layout for this type of card.*

7 *You can customize the publication at a later stage or you can stick with the suggested layout and settings used by the wizard.*

8 *All aspects of the invitation card were defines by the template and we were asked to select various verses.*

9 *You need to save your work much in the same way as you save Word documents.*

10 *There is a range of printing options as some of the publication types will take more than one page.*

22

Making a newsletter, leaflet or pamphlet

In this chapter you will learn
- *how to select a suitable template*
- *working in columns on the page*
- *how to use text and image frames*
- *how to get text to flow from one frame to the next*

You should work through Chapter 21 before attempting this chapter.

22.1 Introduction

Some publications do not require much text, for example, invitations and cards. Other publications such as newsletters and pamphlets require a lot of text. They also tend to be laid out in columns so that the text flows from one column to the next – a bit like a newspaper.

This chapter will focus specifically on publications that use this type of format. The example used will be for a fund-raising newsletter although the skills learned here can be applied to other kinds of publication such as leaflets and pamphlets.

22.2 Getting started

1 *Open Publisher either from the desktop, or from the Start menu. The first screen will offer you the various publication types.*
2 *Select the 'Newsletters' as shown.*

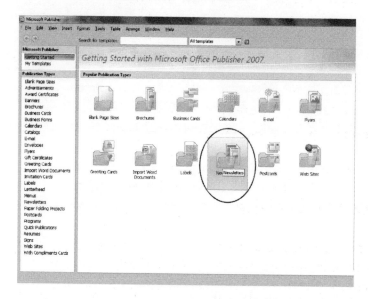

3 *You are now presented with a long list of layout types. You will need to scroll down to see all of the options. Double click on the one called 'Layers'.*

The publication is shown in the main window and some of the options for making changes to it are in the left-hand pane.

Publisher has now presented us with a four-page newsletter and it is displaying page 1. You can tell this because of the small page references in the bottom left of the screen called 'Page navigation':

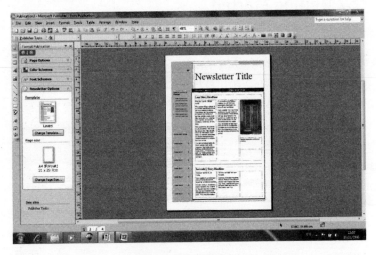

The advantage of using these layouts is that Publisher does a lot of the work for you. However, there is still a lot left to do, as all of the text and images need customizing.

22.3 Changing the text

Publisher uses frames. A frame can contain text or images. It uses frames because it is easier to move the frames around to create the desired layout. When you use Word, the text just appears on the page. In Publisher, text needs to be put in a frame. When you use one of Publisher's designs, some text is put into the frames already, so that you can see what it will look like.

To change the text:

1 *Click in the frame that contains the text. In this case, click in the frame at the top of the publication.*

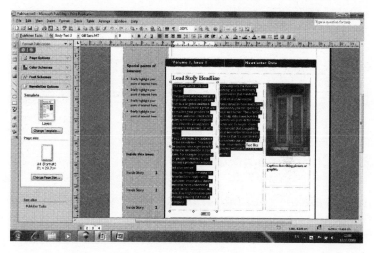

2 *All of the text in that frame is then highlighted. You can now type in the text that you want to appear in this part of the publication.*

The principle is the same now for any of the text frames. Remember you can use F9 to zoom in to make it easier to see what you are typing. Pressing F9 will zoom you out again so you can see the whole of the publication.

22.4 Formatting text

When you were using Word, you got used to the idea of changing the style and size of the font. You can do this within Publisher too in a similar way.

1 *Click on the frame that contains the text you want to change.*
2 *From the toolbar at the top, select the font style and size that you want.*
3 *You can also change the font colour on this toolbar.*

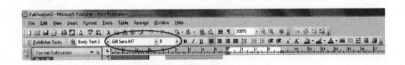

22.5 Changing an image

Images are also put into frames. When you use one of Publisher's designs it will put in some images for you. These are from the ClipArt library. You can put your own image in either by:

▶ *selecting a different ClipArt image*
▶ *copying and pasting an image from somewhere else*
▶ *inserting an image from a file.*

To change a ClipArt image:

1 *Double click on the frame that contains the image. The ClipArt library will now load.*

2 *Search and select another image and insert it as described in Chapter 7.*

3 *Close the ClipArt library. The new image is now inserted.*

To copy and paste an image:

1 *Locate the image that you want to use. For example, you may have found a suitable image on a web page. Right click on it and select 'Copy'.*

2 *Right click in the publication on the image that you want to replace, and click 'Paste'. The image in the frame will be replaced with the new image.*

To insert an image stored in a file:

1 *Click once on the image in the publication that you want to replace.*

2 *Select 'Insert' from the menu and select 'Picture' and 'From File'.*

3 *You can now select an image from your Pictures folder. This will replace the image in the frame.*

22.6 Moving and re-sizing images

Publisher uses what is called text wrapping. This means that it will automatically move text to fit around an image. If you move an image or re-size it, the text will automatically adjust itself.

To re-size an image:

1 *Click on it.*
2 *Move the mouse pointer to one of the four corners of the image until the mouse pointer changes to a diagonal arrow.*
3 *Left click and hold and then drag the corner so that the image re-sizes.*
4 *When you have achieved the size you want, let go of the left mouse button.*

To move an image:

1 *Click on the image and hold onto the mouse button.*
2 *While holding the left mouse button down, move the picture to its new location and then release the left mouse button.*

An alternative to this is to use the arrow keys on the keyboard to move an image. This can be useful as it is a little more precise than using the mouse.

1 *Click on the image.*
2 *Use the ARROW KEYS in the direction that you want the image to move.*

You will notice that the image moves by very small amounts allowing you to position it exactly where you want it.

22.7 Flowing text

This layout uses columns like a standard newspaper. The way we read these is to read to the end of column 1, then start at the top of column 2 and so on.

The text in the three columns is linked together so that if you add more text, it will adjust itself to fit across the columns.

For example:

1 *Click on the column to the left of the image as shown:*

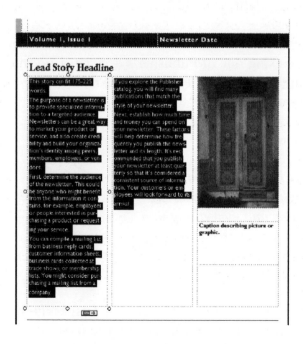

2 *Notice how two columns become highlighted. This is because these two text frames are linked together. Press F9 to zoom in.*

3 *Press the LEFT ARROW KEY on the keyboard. This moves the cursor to the start of this text so that you can edit it.*

4 *Type in 'This is an experiment to show how the text flows between the three columns'.*

As you do this, you will notice that the text is continually adjusting itself so that it can fit in everything you are typing.

22.8 Deleting frames

It may be that you want to delete complete frames. If you are using one of Publisher's designs, as in this case, you might find that there are whole frames that you just don't want.

To delete them:

1 *Click on the frame.*

2 *Right click and press DELETE. This will delete the frame and everything in it.*

22.9 Adding frames

It may be that you need to add new frames. Perhaps you want to add a new image, or you have run out of space in one of the text boxes.

To add a text frame:

1 *Click on the 'A' icon on the left-hand side of the screen as shown.*

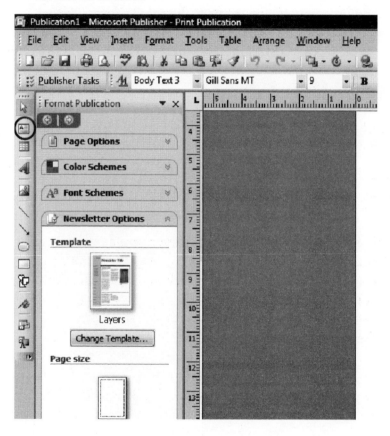

2 *Move the mouse pointer onto the publication wherever you want this new text frame to go. Click and hold the left mouse button while dragging out the frame.*

3 *When you have got the frame the size you want it, release the left mouse button.*

4 *Move the text frame if the location is not quite right.*

Adding a new image frame is the same process except you click on the 'Image' icon rather than the A as shown.

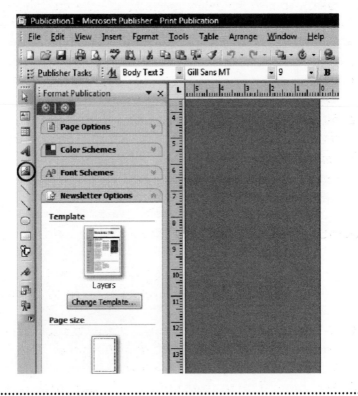

Hints and tips

If you find that you are making lots of changes to one of the standard layouts, you might be better off starting your publication from scratch as described in the next chapter.

22.10 Deleting pages

You may also wish to delete whole pages. For example, this template provided you with a four-page newsletter. It may be that you only want a single page. If this is the case, you need to delete pages 2, 3 and 4 completely.

To do this:

1 *Go to page 2 by clicking on the 'Page navigation' icon in the bottom left-hand corner.*
2 *Now select 'Edit' from the menu option across the top.*
3 *Select 'Delete Page'.*

4 *As there are two pages here it will ask you whether you want to delete one or both of the pages. Select 'Both pages' and click 'OK'.*
5 *You can follow the same process for any further pages you wish to delete.*

IMPORTANT THINGS TO REMEMBER FROM THIS CHAPTER

1 *Publisher has a wide range of publication types.*

2 *We used one of the pre-set templates that has already done much of the work for us.*

3 *One of the types of frame that Publisher uses is a text frame. You can position frames around each other to create a professional looking newsletter.*

4 *Text can be formatted in all of the same ways as in Word, so you can change the size, colour, and style.*

5 *You can also add images. Images go inside image frames in Publisher.*

6 *You can resize and move any of the frames at any time. For example you may want to move an image so that the text flows around it.*

7 *Text can flow automatically from one frame to another. This is particularly useful with a layout which has several columns.*

8 *Whichever frame you type into, Publisher will spread the text across to fill the three columns.*

9 *You can add and delete your own frames. Many people start from a templates rather than having to add all the frames from scratch.*

10 *You can also add or delete whole pages if you want to.*

23

Making a poster

In this chapter you will learn
- *how to design and create a new publication from scratch*
- *how to add text frames*
- *how to add WordArt frames*
- *how to add ClipArt and Picture frames*

23.1 Introduction

This chapter will start from scratch with a blank page onto which you add what you want. It is possible to create a poster using one of the publication types described in Chapters 21 and 22, but for the purposes of this chapter, a blank publication will be used.

As you know Publisher uses frames, so the basic rule is that you add the frame (box) first, and then you put the text or image into the frame.

23.2 Getting started

1 *Open Publisher either from the desktop, or from the Start menu.*

2 *The first screen will offer you the publication types. Select the 'Blank Page Size' option as shown.*

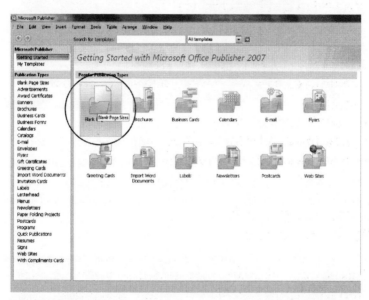

3 *You are now prompted to select the page format. Double click on 'A4 portrait'. You will see that you are presented with a blank publication onto which you can put anything you like.*

Hints and tips

This example is for an A4-sized poster. It is possible to create larger posters using the 'Poster' option. This will print over several pages of A4 and then you have to assemble it yourself.

This poster will be for an up-coming play, which will take place in the village hall. It will include a title, some images and some text explaining what the play is all about. The finished poster is shown here, so this is what you are working towards.

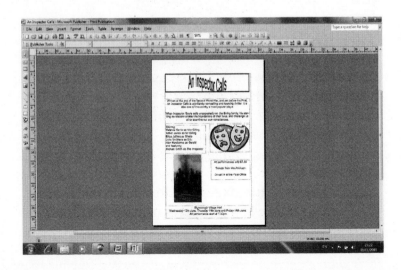

23.3 Adding a title using WordArt

To start with, add the title. This is using WordArt, which is available in all Microsoft software and allows you to create visual effects with words.

1 *Click on the 'WordArt' icon on the right-hand side of the screen as shown below.*

2 *Move the mouse pointer across the top of the page and left click and hold while you drag out a frame big enough to fit in the title. Don't worry if you don't get the size quite right as you can always re-size it later on.*

Use the light blue border as a guide. These allow
room for a white margin around the printed page.

3 *The WordArt options will be displayed. Click on
the one you want and click OK.*

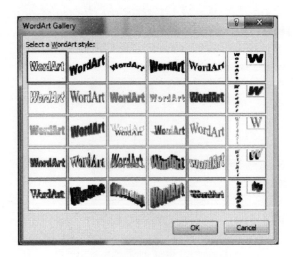

4 *Where it reads 'Your Text Here', type in the title.
In this case: 'An Inspector Calls'.*
5 *Click OK.*

23.4 Adding text frames

The details about the play are contained within a
number of text boxes. You will need to add these boxes
roughly in the positions shown and then add the text
to them.

To add a text box:

1 *Click on the text frame tool on the toolbar on the left-hand side.*

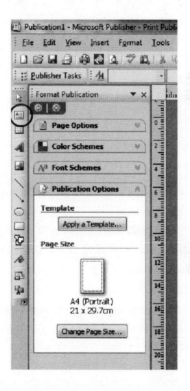

2 *Position the mouse pointer on the page, left click and drag out a text box roughly to the right size, then release the mouse button.*

3 *If you want to adjust the size or location afterwards, you can.*

4 *Type in the text.*

5 *Re-size the text frame so that the text fits neatly in it.*

6 *Change the font to Arial by selecting it and then selecting the Arial font from the list as shown and set the size to 14 (see the next screenshot).*

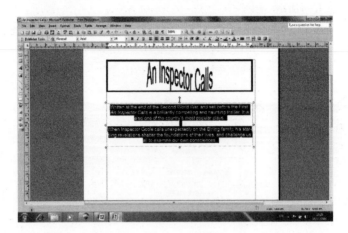

7 *Make sure that you can still read all of the text. Publisher will warn you if the frame is too small to fit in all of the text.*

8 *Centre the text in the middle of the frame by highlighting it and clicking on the 'centre alignment' icon on the toolbar.*
9 *Add any further text frames that you need and then type the text into them. In this example, there are three more text frames: one for the actors, one for*

the dates and times, and one for the prices. Notice that:

▸ *The text frames containing information on dates and times and the prices have been formatted to Arial font size 14 and the text has been centred.*

▸ *The text frames containing the information on actors is formatted to Arial font size 14.*

Hints and tips

Remember that you can use the F9 key at any point to zoom in and out.

Obviously you can choose any font styles and sizes you like in your posters. Bear in mind that this is likely to be stuck up on a notice board somewhere so needs to have a big enough font size for people to read.

23.5 Adding images

There are two images used in this example. One is a ClipArt image and the other is a copyright-free image found on the Internet.

The process of adding images is similar to adding text in that you must first add the frames. To add the ClipArt image:

1 *Select the 'Picture Frame tool' icon from the toolbar on the left-hand side and select 'ClipArt'.*

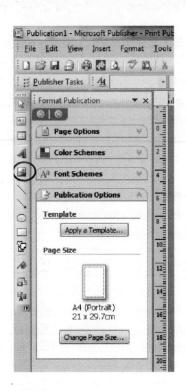

2 *The ClipArt library is now displayed on the left-hand side and you can search for a suitable image as described in Chapter 7.*

Hints and tips

The contents of the ClipArt library can vary depending on what version of Publisher you have. This image might not be available on your computer.

To add a photograph:

1 *Select the 'Picture frame tool' icon from the toolbar on the left and then select 'Picture from file'.*

2 *Drag out a frame into the correct position.*
3 *Go onto the Internet and find a suitable image. Alternatively, if you already have an image yourself, you can use the 'Insert', 'Picture' and 'From File' options.*
4 *When you have found the image, right click on it and select 'Copy'.*
5 *Click in the picture frame that you have just put in, and right click and select 'Paste'. The image will be pasted into the frame and you can re-size it if necessary.*

23.6 Adjusting the layout

The final poster should now be looking something like the one shown earlier. Remember that you can make changes to any part at any time. You can:

▶ *move frames*
▶ *re-size frames*
▶ *add and remove text from frames*
▶ *delete complete frames and add new ones*
▶ *change the font style, size and colour ...*

... and you already know how to do all of these things!

Another useful feature is that you can put borders around each individual frame. To put a border around any of the frames you first need to select the frame that you want to work with.

1 *If you find that you cannot click on a frames, click on the small arrow in the top left-hand corner. This allows you to select objects. Now right click on the frame you want to work with.*

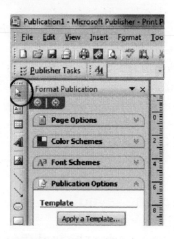

2 *Select 'Format Text Box'.*
3 *In this window you can select 'Line' colour and style or experiment with some pre-set borders using 'BorderArt'.*

You can use this same method to add 'fill' colours to frames as well. This means that they will have a background colour in the frame:

1 *Right click on the frame you want to work with.*
2 *Select 'Format Text Box'.*
3 *Select 'Fill Color'.*
4 *A small number of colours are shown. These will include any colours currently being used in the publication.*

5 *Select 'More Colors'. You can now choose any colour you like by clicking somewhere in the spectrum of colours being shown and some different fill effects.*

6 *Click 'OK' when you have chosen.*

Use of colour will make your poster stand out more, but bear in mind that it will use up your ink cartridges quite quickly.

When you have finished, make sure you save your work. Publisher will have prompted you to save by now anyway. Then you can click on the cross to close Publisher.

Hints and tips

Remember that many of the options that you have used in Word are also available in Publisher so don't be afraid to experiment a bit.

IMPORTANT THINGS TO REMEMBER FROM THIS CHAPTER

1 *In this chapter we started with a blank page and then added the frames to create a publication from scratch, rather than using a template.*

2 *It is useful to have an idea of how you want the final publication to look before you start, so that you have something to work towards.*

3 *WordArt is a feature that allows you to add artistic effects to letters, e.g. curved text. This is particularly useful for headings and titles.*

4 *Text can be edited in the same way that you have seen in Word. In this example, text was centred across the page, which is suitable for a poster.*

5 *ClipArt can be used to add cartoon style pictures and photographs.*

6 *ClipArt only has a limited range of photographs so you may need to go onto the Internet to find more suitable images.*

7 *You can adjust the size and location of any of the frames to create the overall effect that you are after.*

8 *To work with an individual frame, you click on it first to make sure that it is highlighted.*

9 *You can also change the colour of the frames and the style of the borders.*

10 *You can overlap frames if you want to.*

24

Keeping track of your personal finances

In this chapter you will learn
- *the basics of Microsoft Excel spreadsheet software*
- *how to type text and numbers into 'cells'*
- *how to carry out automatic calculations*
- *how to update your spreadsheets*
- *how to print spreadsheets*

24.1 Introduction

Spreadsheet software is designed specifically to work with numbers. It can be used for any job where you need to carry out calculations of figures. It is much more than a calculator though, as you can set up spreadsheets that will work automatically. In this example, we will create a spreadsheet of personal finances for the month. Once it has been set up, all you have to do next month is update the figures, and the whole thing updates automatically.

24.2 Spreadsheet basics

The easiest way to understand a spreadsheet is to look at one.

Double click on 'Microsoft Excel' from your desktop, or if you don't have a link on your desktop, click on 'Start', 'All Programs' and find it in the list.

Excel will open and you will see this screen:

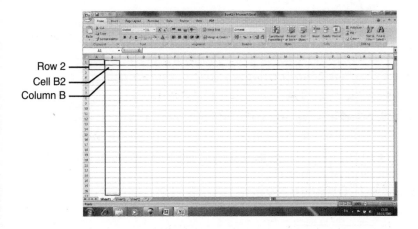

Row 2
Cell B2
Column B

As you can see, you are faced with a large grid made up of columns and rows. Across the top of the grid there are letters (for each column) and down the left-hand side, there are numbers (for each row). Each small box in the grid is called a cell. Each cell can be referenced using the letters and numbers. For example, B2 is the cell reference where column B and row 2 meet.

> **Hints and tips**
>   Think of the letters and numbers like coordinates
>   on a map. If you have ever played the game
>   Battleships, it is exactly the same principle being
>   used here.

There are only three things that you can type into
each cell:

▶ *Text: normal text can be typed in so that you
  can add titles and labels, e.g. 'Finances for
  June'.*
▶ *Numbers: the numbers that you want to calculate,
  e.g. all of your monthly expenses.*
▶ *Formulae: these are calculations, e.g. adding up all
  of your monthly expenses to get a total.*

We are now going to work through a typical example
setting up a spreadsheet that records all the money
coming in and going out of a typical household for the
period of a month.

24.3 Adding text to a spreadsheet

First, we need to put a clear title on the spreadsheet:

1 *Click in cell A1.*
2 *Type 'Monthly Budget' as shown on the screen
  below. Notice how the title goes across cells A1 and
  B1. This does not matter at this stage.*

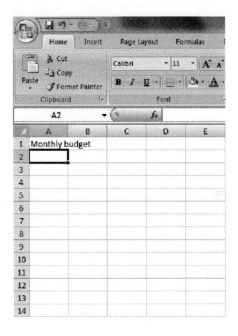

3 *In cell A3, type 'Outgoings'. We are going to use column A to list all of the items that you have to pay for every month (e.g. gas bills, food bills, etc.).*

4 *Click in cell A4. Now type the first of your outgoings (e.g. Gas).*

5 *Click in cell A5 and type the next outgoing (e.g. Electricity).*

6 *Keep going until you have listed all of your outgoings. Your spreadsheet will now look something like this:*

Hints and tips

Row 2 has been left blank just to make the spreadsheet easier to read. You can lay out your spreadsheet however you like.

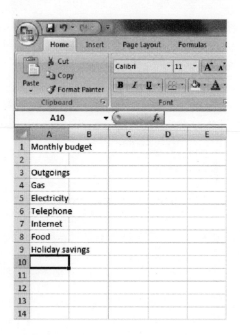

24.4 Making the columns wider

Some of the descriptions are too wide to fit in the cells and they are taking up column A and column B. Column A needs to be wide enough to fit in the longest title. To do this, you can drag the column out using the mouse:

1 *Locate the mouse pointer in between the letters A and B.*
2 *The pointer will change to a line with two arrows pointing left and right. Hold down the left mouse button and move the mouse to the right. You will see that the column gets wider.*

3 *Widen the column until it is wide enough to include the longest description in your list, then let go of the left button.*

An alternative is to double click when the mouse pointer changes. This will adjust the width of the column automatically to fit all the text in.

Hints and tips

If you find it tricky to widen columns with the mouse, try this: Right click on the column and select 'Column Width' from the menu. The width is measured in the number of characters.

24.5 Adding numbers to a spreadsheet

We are now going to use column B to type in the numbers. In this case, it will be the value in pounds of each item.

1 *Click in cell B4 and type 50. Don't worry about the pound signs just yet.*
2 *Now complete the rest of column B typing in all the values. As this will be pounds and pence, you can type in values such as 52.34 if you want to be precise.*

24.6 Formatting numbers to currency

All of the values in column B need to be shown as pounds and pence. To do this:

1 *Select all of the cells from B4 to B10. You do this by positioning the mouse pointer in cell B4 and holding down the left mouse button. Then move the mouse down until you get to cell B10 and let go of the mouse button. You will see the cells go grey showing you that you are selecting them.*

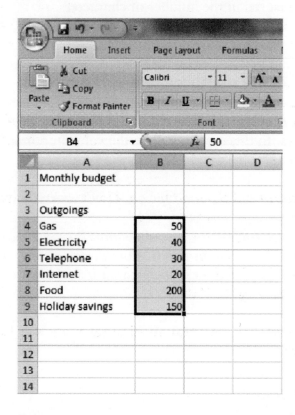

2 *With the cells selected, click on the little arrow just to the right of the box that reads 'General' as shown.*

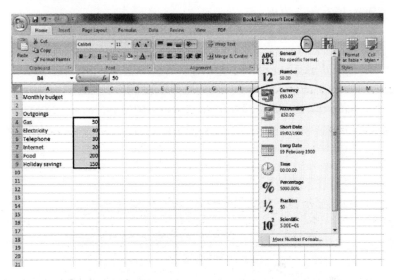

3 *Select 'Currency' from the list. It is set to UK pounds so assuming that is what you want, click on 'OK'.*

You will see that all of the values in column B are now showing a pounds and pence.

24.7 Using formulae

The next step is to total up all of the outgoings for the month.

1 *Click in cell A10 and type 'Total outgoings'.*
2 *So far we have typed text and numbers. We now need to use a formula to add up all of the outgoings.*
3 *Click in cell B10.*
4 *Click on the autosum icon, which you will find on the top right-hand side of the screen. Excel assumes that you want to add up all the values in column B and it will put these into a sum for you. In this case, the sum it does is:*

=SUM(B4:B9)

This means that it will sum (add up) all of the values in the cells from B4 to B9 as shown.

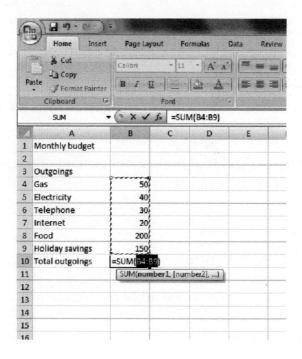

4 *Press ENTER. It will now show the total value in cell B10.*

The next step is to add any further text, numbers or formulae that are needed. In this case, it means putting in all of the money coming in each month. You could do this further down column A, or use the other columns. In this example, we have used columns D and E:

Hints and tips

There are hundreds of columns and thousands of rows so you are never going to run out. To keep scrolling to a minimum, try to design your spreadsheets so that they fit onto one screen full.

1 *Type 'Income' into cell D3 as shown:*

2 *You will need to widen column D and format column E to Currency as previously described. In cell D11, type 'Total Income' as shown. It has been put here so that it is in the same row as the Total outgoings.*

3 *Click in E11 and click on the autosum button. Excel has guessed at which cells you want to add up, but this time, it has got it wrong.*

4 *Click in cell E11 and change the formula so that it reads =SUM(E4:E6). To do this, point the mouse between the E and the 11 and click. Delete the 11 and put 6 instead.*

5 *Press ENTER. The Total income value is now shown.*

6 *The final stage is to do a calculation to see how much money you have left each month. In cell A13, type 'Money left'.*

7 *In cell B13, type '=E11-B11'. This will take the value in B11 (Total outgoings) away from the value in E11 (Total income) to show you the money you have left.*

24.8 Saving your spreadsheet

At this stage, you are probably thinking that you could have done all of this much quicker on a calculator – and you might be right. However, the beauty of spreadsheets is that once you have set one up, you can use them over and over again. All you need to do next month is change the figures, and all of the calculations will update automatically.

To do this:

1 *Click on the Microsoft Office icon in the very top left-hand corner and select 'Save', or click on the 'Save icon' in the Quick Access toolbar.*
2 *The file save window is now displayed and it is set up to put things into the folder called Documents. You can change to a different folder if you have set one up, or save it here.*
3 *Where it says 'File Name' at the bottom, type in 'June Finances'.*

This will save the file as June Finances in the Documents folder. This is where it will be if you want to open it again at a later stage. You can safely close the file now.

24.9 Updating a spreadsheet

Let's now assume a month has passed and we want to do our finances for July.

1 *Open the June Finances file (it may already be open).*
2 *In cells B4 to B10 you can change the outgoings for July. In cells E4 to E6, you can change the income figures for July.*

It is important that you do not change the values in any cell where you have done a formula, as these do not need changing. For example, let's say that the food bill went up this month to £150:

3 *Click in cell B8 and type in '150'. Look in cells B11, E11 and B13 where all the totals are calculated. They have changed automatically as a result of the change you made in cell B8.*

Hints and tips

This is where a spreadsheet can really save you time as once you have set them up, you can change the figures and all of the totals will re-calculate automatically.

You now need to save this file with a new name:

1 *Click on the Microsoft Office icon in the very top left-hand corner and select 'Save As' from the menu options. This will save the file with a new name.*
2 *As before, the standard folder for saving your work is called Documents.*
3 *Where it says 'File Name' at the bottom, type in 'July Finances'. This means that the June Finances file will still be there in case you ever need it again and you will have a new file called July Finances.*

You can repeat this process each month creating a whole archive of files.

24.10 Making spreadsheets look attractive

Spreadsheets are mainly used for (boring) financial stuff and it is usually sufficient for them to be fairly plain in terms of the layout. In the example above, we left a row spare and lined up our totals to make it a bit easier to read. Apart from that, the layout was a bit dull.

There are things that you can do to liven up spreadsheets a bit. You can:

▸ *Add colour to the text, the cell backgrounds and borders.*
▸ *Change font styles and sizes.*
▸ *Add borders around cells.*

The process for doing any of these things is quite similar so you might want to experiment with them a bit.

Start by selecting the cells that you want to change. For example, to change the font in all the cells on the June Finances spreadsheet:

1 *Select all of the cells from A1 to F13. Do this by clicking in cell A1 and holding down the left mouse button while moving it across to F13. When you get to F13, release the left mouse button.*
2 *Now that the cells are selected, under the Home tab at the top of the screen you will find the options to change the font. This is exactly the same as in Word.*

3 *You can now change the font size and style.*

To apply changes to specific cells, click on the individual cell rather than selecting a range of cells. For example, to highlight the title in blue:

1 *Click on cell A1.*
2 *Click on the 'Font color' icon.*
3 *Select one of the blues and the colour of the text in cell A1 will change to blue.*
4 *The other options here are the cell fill colour which colours in, the cell and the border option, which will put a border around cells to make them stand out.*

All of these options work in the same way. The bold and italic options can also be applied in exactly the same way as in Word. Select the cell or range of cells that you want to change, and then click on the option that you want to apply.

This final image shows a more attractive spreadsheet that has been created simply by using bold text and borders to highlight the important cells, and increasing the font size of the titles.

IMPORTANT THINGS TO REMEMBER FROM THIS CHAPTER

1 *Excel is an example of spreadsheet software and is designed to work with numbers.*

2 *Spreadsheets can be set up with mathematical formulae. Once you have set one up for a task, you can use it over and over again.*

3 *Spreadsheets are made up of columns, rows and cells, identified by letters and numbers.*

4 *There are only three things you can type into a cell: text, numbers and formulae.*

5 *You can format the text in the same way that you do in Word or Publisher. You may have to adjust the column widths to fit it all in.*

6 *You can format numbers according to what they represent. For example, you might what to format numbers as currency.*

7 *Formulae are used to carry out calculations. For example, you could use a formula to add up your total expenses each month.*

8 *Once you have set up a formula, the spreadsheet will re-calculate automatically if any of the numbers used in the formula change.*

9 *You can format the spreadsheet to look professional, e.g. by shading in the cells, or adding borders.*

10 *You can save your spreadsheets and use them over and over again.*

25

....

Keeping track of your investments

In this chapter you will learn
- *how to calculate values using percentages in Excel*
- *how to type in formulae*
- *how to copy and paste formulae between cells*
- *how to wrap text within a cell*
- *how to create graphs*

25.1 Introduction

If you have personal savings accounts, bonds or shares, then you will know the value of these investments. Each month you might want to calculate how much money you can expect to receive in interest or dividends. You might also want to track the total value of your shares if you were considering selling them.

This chapter will show you how to set up a spreadsheet to do this and show you how to produce a graph so that you visualize the return on your investment.

25.2 Setting up the spreadsheet

You might want to type in your own figures for your own investments, or you can work through the example provided here.

1 *Open the Excel software by double clicking on the icon from the desktop, or from the Start menu.*
2 *You are presented with an empty worksheet made up of many cells.*
3 *In cell A1, type in a title, for example: My Investments.*
4 *List your investments in column A or copy the example below. Notice that we have split out the savings from the shares.*

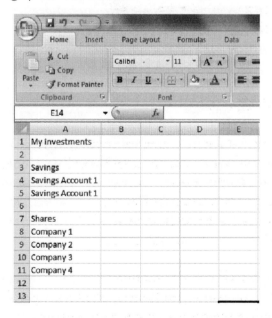

We are now going to add some column headings for the information that we need to know about each investment. Below them we will type the column headings for the shares.

1 *In cell B3, type 'Amount saved'.*
2 *In cell C3, type 'Interest rate'.*
3 *In cell D3, type 'Interest gained'.*
4 *In cell B7, type 'Number of shares'.*
5 *In cell C7, type 'Price paid per share'.*
6 *In cell D7, type 'Current price per share'.*
7 *In cell E7, type 'Total paid'.*
8 *In cell E8, type 'Total value now'.*
9 *You will need to widen the columns to get the titles in.*

25.3 Wrapping text

When you type into word processing software such as Word, you get to the end of the line and the cursor automatically moves to the start of the next line. This is called wrapping. We can use wrapping in Excel too. You might have noticed that the columns are getting quite wide so that the text fits in. Using text wrapping, we can split the text over more than one line in each cell.

1 *Select cells A7 to F7 by doing a left click and hold on cell A7 and then dragging the mouse pointer to F7 and letting go.*
2 *Click on 'Wrap text' as shown.*
3 *Now make the columns narrower and the rows deeper. As you do this, you will see that the text is wrapping over two lines as shown.*

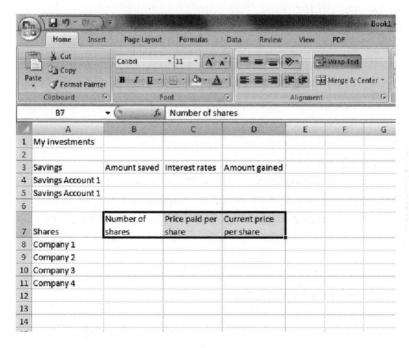

25.4 Entering the numbers and formulae for the savings

Now that all the headings are set up, you can type in the values.

1 *In cells B4 and B5, type in the total amount of money in each savings account, in this example 50000 and 23000.*
2 *Format these two cells to currency as shown in the previous chapter.*
3 *In cells C4 and C5, type in the percentage interest rate, in this case 5% and 4.75%. It is very important that you type the percentage (%) sign (SHIFT and 5) so that Excel knows this is a percentage.*
4 *In cell B4, a formula is needed to work out how much interest has been gained. This will be B4*C4. Because we are doing monthly figures, it also needs to be divided by 12 as the interest rate is annual. In cell B4, type =B4*C4/12.*

Hints and tips

The multiply sign is the asterisk (*). There is a key for it in the number pad on the right-hand side of your keyboard or you can use SHIFT and 8. The divide key is a slash. There is one in the number pad and one towards the bottom right-hand side of the main keyboard.

5 *The amount of interest earned is now displayed. Format this to currency in the usual way. This will add the £ sign and limit the number to two decimal places.*

6 *Rather than typing the formula again in D5, you can copy the formula from D4 to D5. To do this, right click on cell D4 and select 'Copy'. Then click on cell D5 and right click and select 'Paste'.*

The formula is copied and Excel cleverly changes it so that it is =B5*C5/12. Also, because the format of the cell was currency, it copies the format into the new cell.

25.5 Entering the numbers and formulae for the shares

The numbers and formulae needed to calculate how much the shares are worth is different.

First, you need to enter the numbers as shown in this screenshot.

1 *In cells B8 to B11, type in the number of shares held in each company. In this example: B8 is 5000, B9 is 1000, B10 is 300 and B11 is 200.*

2 *In cells C8 to C11, type in the amount that was paid for each individual share. In this example: C8 is £2.50, C9 is £4.00, C10 is £1.50 and C11 is £1.32.*

3 *In cells D8 to D11, type in the current price of each share. In this example: D8 is £2.53, D9 is £4.50, D10 is £1.25 and D11 is £1.43.*

	B	C	D	E	F	G	H
	J16		f_x				
2							
3	Amount saved	Interest rate	Interest gained				
4	£ 50,000.00	5%	£ 208.33				
5	£ 23,000.00	4.75%	£ 91.04				
6							
7	Number of shares	Price paid per share	Current price per share	Total paid	Total value now		
8	5000	£ 2.50	£ 2.53				
9	1000	£ 4.00	£ 4.50				
10	300	£ 1.50	£ 1.25				
11	200	£ 1.32	£ 1.43				
12							
13							
14							
15							

Columns E and F need formulae in them as they can be calculated from the other columns.

4 *In cell E8, type =B8*C8. This is the total amount spent on shares in Company 1. Format this to currency in the usual way.*

5 *In cell F8, type =D8*D8. This is the total amount that the shares would be worth if you sold them now. Format this to currency in the usual way.*

Hints and tips

You can go on forever with spreadsheets. For example, you could add another formula in column G to work out the difference between columns E and F, or you could add subtotals in row 12.

25.6 Copying formulae across cells

There are just a few cells left to fill in. You could type in the formula as described previously. However, as the formulae needed are all basically the same, you can copy the existing formulae into the blank cells. For example, the formulae needed in cells E9 to E11 are basically the same as the one used in cell E8. The formulae needed in cells F9 to F11 are basically the same as the one used in cell F8.

Let's start by copying the formula into E9 to E11:

1 *Click in cell E8.*
2 *Move the mouse pointer into the bottom right-hand corner of cell E8 until the mouse pointer changes to a small black cross.*
3 *Now hold down the left button on the mouse and move the mouse down so that you are selecting cells E9, E10 and E11.*
4 *Then let go of the left mouse button. The formula has now been copied down into these cells and Excel has automatically changed it so that it refers to the correct cell references.*
5 *You now need to do exactly the same thing copying the formula in F8 to cells F9, F10 and F11.*
6 *Your spreadsheet is now complete. Save it and give it a sensible name, for example: My Investments.*

Remember that you can come back and change this spreadsheet at any time. For example, if interest rates change, or if share prices change, you can type in the new values and the spreadsheet will recalculate all your figures automatically.

25.7 Creating a graph

A graph or chart is a visual way of looking at data. It can be easier to look at a graph and understand what is happening rather than looking at rows and rows of numbers.

Hints and tips

Like other things in Excel, once you have set up your graph, it will change automatically if any of the numbers change.

First you need to decide what you want to create a graph of. A useful graph in this example would be to plot the 'Total paid' and 'Total value now' values to see whether each company has made you any money or not.

The first step is to select the cells that you want to plot. As well as selecting the cells, you also need to select the text, as Excel is clever enough to put these onto the graph for you as the axes labels.

1 *Select cells A7 to A11 by clicking and holding on A7 and then dragging the mouse down to A11.*
2 *Hold down the CTRL key and select cells E7 to F11 in exactly the same way. You will notice that A7 to A11 remain selected and that all the cells from E7 to F11 are also selected.*

Hints and tips

Holding down the CTRL key allows you to select groups of cells that are not next to each other in the spreadsheet. This is very useful when you just want to graph certain values, as in this case.

3 *Click on the 'Insert' tab at the top of the screen. You will see a range of chart options as shown below:*

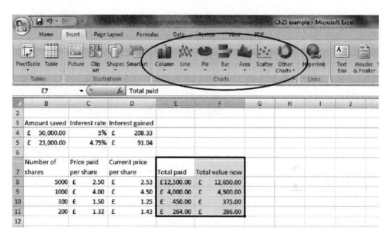

4 *Click on column chart and select the type of column chart you want from the list. In this case a 2D chart is used.*

5 *The graph is now shown in your spreadsheet. You can click on it and drag it around, putting it wherever you want on the page. You can also re-size it by clicking on one of the corners and dragging to a larger or smaller size.*

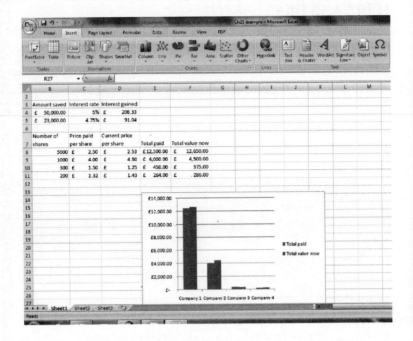

6 *In this case, drag the graph just below all of the figures as there is room for both with the graph at the current size.*

7 *Save your file again.*

If you change any of the values for the shares in the cells, you will notice that the graph updates itself automatically.

IMPORTANT THINGS TO REMEMBER FROM THIS CHAPTER

1 *You can use spreadsheets in any situation where you need to carry out some calculations on an ongoing basis.*

2 *You can wrap text within a cell. This means that if you have a lot of text, you can make the column narrower and the text will adjust itself to fit.*

3 *There are a number of ways of formatting numbers in addition to currency. For example, you can show numbers as percentages.*

4 *When working out a formula, the trick is to think about how you would do it with a calculator and then re-create this as a formula in Excel.*

5 *You can use all the standard mathematical operators such as + - / and * plus there are many other functions you could experiment with.*

6 *Where you are using the same formula over and over again, it is possible to copy it instead of having to retype it.*

7 *A range of graphs are available in Excel including line graphs, pie charts and bar charts.*

8 You *have to highlight the cells that you want to plot on the graph and Excel will create the chart for you automatically.*

9 You *can reposition the graph anywhere on the spreadsheet.*

10 You *should format your spreadsheet in a way that makes it easy for you to read off the information you need.*

26

Keeping lists of names and addresses

In this chapter you will learn
- *how to use Microsoft Access database software*
- *how to set up a database of names and addresses*
- *how to add, change and remove information in a database*
- *how to search for information stored in a database*
- *how to sort a database*

26.1 Introduction

A database is a collection of related information. For example, your doctor's surgery will have a database that lists all of the patients and details about them; every time you receive a piece of junk mail through the post, it is because you are on a database somewhere.

Databases can be useful for personal use as well. One of the common uses is to set up a database of all of the people in your address/phone book. In this sense, a database is an electronic version of your address book. If you are involved in running a club or society, a database could be really useful for storing contact details of all the members and other useful information, such as whether they have paid their subs!

Databases are made up of fields and records. A field is one piece of information that is stored on the database. For example, on a doctor's surgery database the fields might be patient name, name of their doctor, date of last appointment, drugs prescribed, etc. A record is a collection of fields for one person. For example, your medical record is all of the information about you.

If you have worked through the chapters on spreadsheets, it is easiest to think of fields as columns and records as rows.

26.2 Getting started

The most common database software for home computer users (and for many businesses too) is Microsoft® Access. Access is a bit different from the other software that we have looked at so far in this book. There are two stages to using Access. The first is to set up the database and the second is to add all of the information.

First, you need to decide what information you want to store. The example used in this chapter will be a database of contact details for friends and families (i.e. your address book). You have to break down each piece of information that you want to store. Each different piece of information is called a field. In this case, we need the following fields:

Title (Mr, Mrs, Ms, Miss, Dr, etc.)
First Name
Last Name
Address
Postcode
Phone Number
Mobile Number
Email Address

1 *Open Access either by double clicking on it from the desktop, or by clicking on 'Start', 'All Programs' and then finding it in the list.*
2 *Select 'Blank Database'. It is possible to download ready-made databases from the Internet from this screen. For example there is one for Contacts and you might like to try this. In this case we will start from scratch and go through all of the options.*

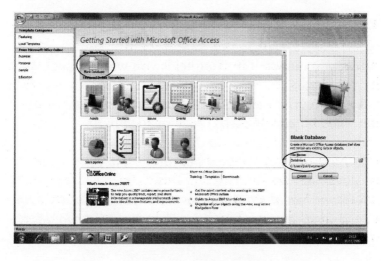

3 *You are then asked to save your database (even though you haven't actually made it yet!). This will be saved into the Documents folder. Where it says 'File Name', type 'My addresses' and click 'Create'.*

4 *Select the 'Create' tab from the top of the screen and select 'Table design'. You will now see a screen that looks like this:*

5 *Click on 'View' and it will prompt you for a name for your table. Type in 'My addresses'.*

First, you must tell it what fields you want to use:

1 *The first of our fields is going to be the title of the person (e.g. Mr, Mrs, etc.) so click in the box that reads 'Field Name' and type 'Title'.*

2 *Now click in the next box down and type 'First Name'.*

3 *Continue like this until you have typed in all of the fields that we identified earlier. Your list should look like this when complete.*

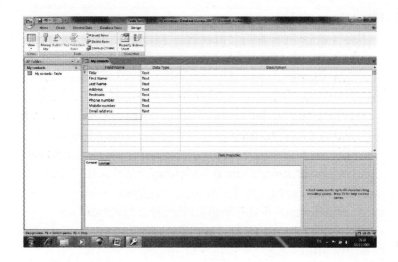

26.3 Setting the correct data types

The data types are quite important. They tell Access how to handle the information that you are going to type in. Text is the most common data type and, as the name suggests, you use it whenever you want to type in letters. You can also use it to type in numbers. This might seem a bit odd, but if you think about the typical address, it might be something like 12 Acacia Avenue. This is actually a mixture of letters and numbers.

Every time you set up a new field it will automatically be set to text. As you can see by looking the data type column.

In fact, all of our fields do need to be set to text. It might seem odd to set Phone Number and Mobile Number to text but you need to do this so that you can add brackets and spaces if you want to. Another reason is that if you set them to number, Access will remove the leading zero at the beginning of a number, for example 01673 343434 becomes 1673343434, which is really annoying.

There is one other useful feature that we will use and this is called the lookup wizard. By now, you have probably filled in a few forms on the computer, usually on the Internet. Often when you are filling in a form, rather than having to type in information, you are given a choice from a list. In Access, creating a list like this is called the lookup column.

It would be useful to set up the Title field as a list as there are only a few choices, e.g. Mr, Mrs, etc. This way, when you are typing the names and addresses, rather than having to type Mr or Mrs, you just choose from the list.

To set this up:

1 *Click in the field that you set up called 'Title'.*
2 *Click on 'Lookup wizard' option under Data Type.*

3 *On the next screen, select the 'I will type in the values that I want' button.*

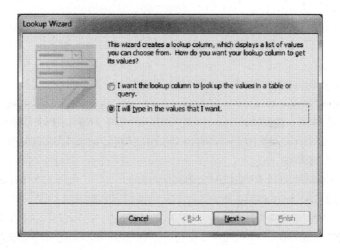

4 *Click 'Next'.*
5 *In 'Col1', type the list of titles that you want to be available to you later on, as shown.*

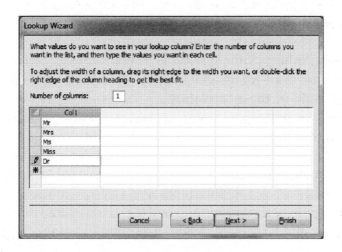

6 *Click 'Next'.*
7 *Click 'Finish'.*

It is not obvious that this has worked, but don't worry, you will see later on when the list appears.

You now need to save these changes:

1 *Click on the Microsoft Office icon and select 'Save' or click on the 'Save' icon on the Quick Access Toolbar.*
2 *Name the table: My addresses.*
3 *You then get a message about a 'primary key'. You can select 'No' on this.*
4 *Close this window by clicking on the cross. Make sure that you close this window, rather than the whole database.*

26.4 Typing in the names and addresses

The first stage of the process is now complete. Your database is all set up and ready to go. You now need to type in all of the information.

To enter the actual names and address into the database you need to be in 'View' mode. This is a bit confusing as Access has a 'Design Mode' used to set up the field names and data types and a 'View' mode where you can type in and view the actual data (names and addresses in this case). 'View' mode

looks a bit like a spreadsheet and works in much the
same way.

1 *Select 'My addresses'.*
2 *To get into View mode, click on the 'View' icon in
 the top left-hand corner of the screen. You can now
 type in the details in the relevant columns. Start
 with the first person.*
3 *Click on the little arrow in the first row of the
 Title column.*

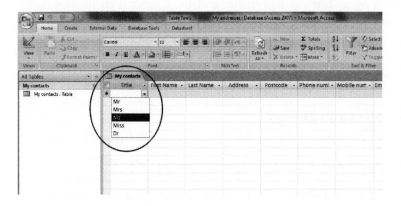

4 *The list that we made earlier is displayed and you
 can choose the appropriate title by clicking on it.*
5 *Click in the First Name cell and type in the person's
 first name.*
6 *Complete the first row.*

You will notice that some of the columns are not wide
enough to display all of the information that you have
typed into them. There are two things you can do about
this. The first is to widen the columns in the same way
that you do in Excel. That is, you move the mouse

pointer to the gap between the field names, click and hold and then drag the mouse to make the columns wider, or narrower.

7 *Take some time to ensure that the columns are the correct width.*

8 *Maximize the window so that it is full screen. Click on the 'maximize' button.*

The example below shows a database table on full screen, with the column widths adjusted to fill the page. A few dummy records have been filled in to show you how it will look. You now need to spend some time working through your address book and typing in all of the details.

Hints and tips

If you do not have certain bits of information, for example if someone does not have a mobile phone number or an email address, just leave it blank. You can always come back and fill it in if they get one at a later date.

26.5 Searching for information

Once you have typed in all of the information, your database is now ready to use. The most likely use for this database is to be able to find someone's details as quickly as possible. You might have lots of records, in which case you don't want to have to scan through them all to find what you want. This is where a database is useful as you can get it to do the searching for you.

You can search in any of the fields. For example, if you wanted to find people called Smith, you would search in the Last Name. To do this:

1   *Click in one of the 'Last Name' records in the table. It does not matter whose record you click on as long as you click on one of the last names.*
2   *Click on the 'Find' icon at the top of the screen as shown.*

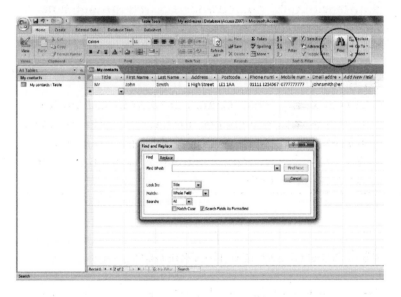

3   *You are now prompted to type in what you are searching for. Type 'Smith' as shown.*
4   *Click on the 'Find Next' button.*
5   *It will quickly search through the records and find the first Smith, highlighting it in black.*

6 *If this is not the Smith you want, click 'Find Next' and it will go to the next one.*

You can use this same method to find anything. The trick is to click on the table in the field that you want to search before clicking the 'Find' button.

This example database had only three records, which is a bit pathetic really. If you had only three names and addresses to enter it would not really be worth making a database in the first place. The real power of databases comes when you have got tens or even hundreds of different records to search through.

26.6 Sorting information into order

In this database, it would be useful to sort the database in alphabetical order based on last name. It might be that if you have copied the information from your address book that it is already in alphabetical order. To make sure that it is in alphabetical order:

1 *Click on the column heading 'Last Name'. When you do this, the whole column is highlighted in black.*

2 *Click on the 'Sort' icon at the top of the screen as shown.*

All of the records will be re-ordered in ascending alphabetical order. This will make it much easier to find the records you are looking for.

26.7 Editing (changing) the database

Information held on your database is likely to change. People might move house, or change their phone numbers or even join the Internet revolution and get themselves an email address!

If this happens, you simply over-type the old information with the new information. For example, if John Smith moved house to 54 The Ridings, Lincoln, you would simply click where the current address is, delete the old address and type in the new one.

To delete a whole record:

1 *Find the record you want to delete.*
2 *Click on the number of the record on the left-hand side. This will highlight the whole row in black.*
3 *Right click and select 'Delete Record'. There is a final warning that you are about to delete the entire row. Click 'Yes'.*

26.8 Printing name and address labels

You may want to print your names and address onto sticky labels, which you can then stick on envelopes. This is particularly useful for sending out cards at Christmas, or if you are involved with a club or society. To do this, you will need to use what is called mail merge. This is actually available in Word, but will use the database that you have set up in Access. We will use the 'My addresses' database set up earlier in this chapter.

1 *Open Word.*
2 *Select the 'Mailing' tab from the options at the top of the screen and select 'Start Mail Merge' and then select 'Step by Step Mail Merge Wizard'*
3 *This will then take you through a series of steps that will create labels ready for printing from the list of names and addresses in your Access database. The wizard is displayed in the right-hand pane as shown. It will ask you a series of questions. You need to answer the questions and then click on Next in the bottom right-hand corner.*
4 *Select 'Labels' and click on 'Next: starting document' in the bottom right hand corner. Note that you can produce other types of documents at this stage.*
5 *The next question is about the layout of the labels on the page. Select 'Insert Merge Field' and select title, first name, last name, address and postcode.*

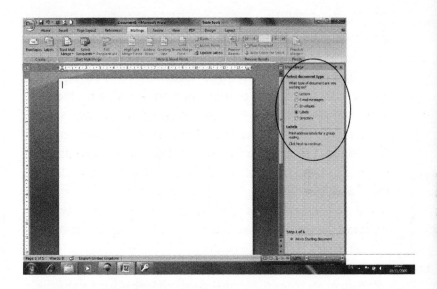

Spend a bit of time arranging these so that they are laid out like an address as shown.

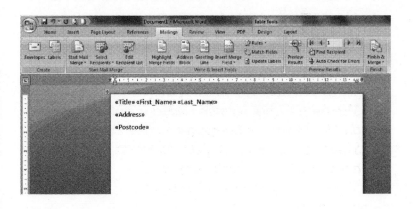

«Title» «First_Name» «Last_Name»

«Address»

«Postcode»

6 *You will be prompted to choose the type of labels you want to use. This will depend on what labels stationery you have bought for your printer. Click 'Next: Select Recipients'.*

7 *Click on 'Use an existing list' and click on 'Browse'. Find your 'My addresses' database. You can spot that it is an Access file as it will have a purple icon.*

8 *Click 'Next: Arrange your labels'. You now have the option of making changes to the layout, but as you have already set up an address block, you can simply click on 'Next: Preview your labels'. The first of your labels is now shown with the full name and address.*

Hints and tips

There are hundreds of different labels to choose from. Make sure you get the right size and the ones that work in your printer.

---

9 *Click on 'Next: Complete the Merge' and the labels will be created for everyone in the database (only three in our example).*

10 *To see all of the labels, select 'Edit individual labels' and you will be able to scroll through all of the labels it has produced. This is a normal Word file and you can make edits to it in the same way as any other Word file.*

11 *When you are happy that it is all OK, select the Microsoft Office icon and select 'Print' or click on the 'Print' icon in the Quick Access Toolbar.*

12 *Save the document as: Address labels. You can now close Word.*

IMPORTANT THINGS TO REMEMBER FROM THIS CHAPTER

1 *A database is a collection of related information. You usually set up databases for a specific reason, e.g. membership details for a club.*

2 *Databases are made up of fields and records. A field is one item of information, e.g. Name. A record is a completed set of fields for one person.*

3 *A database contains one or more tables where the information is stored The structure of the table must be defined before it can be used.*

4 *The first job is to identify and then set up all the fields, in this case, name, address etc.*

5 *You also need to assign the correct data type to each field. In most cases the data type will be 'text'.*

6 *Access uses drop down lists, which show up as little arrows that you click on to reveal a list of options. These make it easier to fill in the database.*

7 *After you have set up and saved the table you have to type in all of the information. This could take some time!*

8 *There are facilities to search and sort information stored in a database.*

9 *You can go back and edit your database at any time as the information changes.*

10 *There is a 'mail merge' feature in Word where you can set it up to create mailing labels or letters to send to everyone in your database.*

27

Creating a slideshow presentation

In this chapter you will learn
- *how to use Microsoft PowerPoint software*
- *how to create a computer-based slideshows*
- *how to add text, images and photographs to your slideshows*
- *how to run a slideshow*

27.1 Introduction

Slideshows can be used to present information to people. If you think about the holiday photographs example above, the photos are transferred onto slides and then the person projects the slides onto a screen one by one while talking about them.

A PowerPoint® slideshow is the modern equivalent of this and can be used where you want to present information to one or more people. It is possible to project computer images onto larger screens using a specialized projector. These are quite expensive and it is not suggested that you go out and buy one just for personal use. However, projectors are common in schools and colleges and are becoming more common in clubs and societies so you might get the chance to use one.

Even without a projector, a slideshow can be presented on the computer screen, which is often sufficient for a smaller audience. Another option is to send people your slideshow so that they can view it on their own computer.

Hints and tips

If you are not talking people through your slideshow, you might need to put more detailed explanations in the text.

27.2 Getting started

1 *Open Microsoft PowerPoint either by double clicking on the icon on your desktop, or by going to the 'Start' menu, 'All Programs' and clicking on it in the list.*
The opening screen will look like the one on the opposite page.

This will be the opening slide of your presentation and is set up to have a title and sub-title on it. One slide will take up one screenful when the slideshow is being shown. Slideshows will contain several slides. The number of slides depends on how long you want the presentation to be.

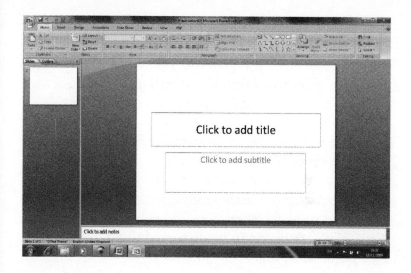

PowerPoint works in much the same way as Word. The main difference is that you are creating a slideshow that will be shown on computer, rather than a document that will be printed out.

Hints and tips

If you are going to present your slides (i.e. talk about them as you show them), a rough rule of thumb is that you need approximately one slide for every three minutes of talk.

The first slide is normally an introduction slide that introduces the topic and the speaker/writer.

The blank area on the left of the screen is an outline view of your slideshow. As you fill in each slide, the text that you type will be shown in this area. This is really useful as you add more and more slides.

The main window is the slide itself and this particular slide has space for a title and a subtitle.

1 *Click where it says 'Click to add title'. You can now type in the name of the presentation. In this example type 'Volunteer Work'.*

2 *Click where it says 'Click to add subtitle' and type your name in here.*

The font size looks massive compared to sizes that you have been using in other chapters. However, this is because it is designed to be presented to a group so the font needs to be big.

Notice how the outline view on the left of the screen also shows the text that you have typed in. You can edit the slide here as well if you want to.

27.3 Adding more slides

You are now ready to add more slides:

1 *Under the 'Home' tab at the top of the screen, click on 'New slide'. The following options are displayed:*

2 *This shows you different layouts that you can choose from.*

3 *Select the layout called 'Title and Content'. This slide is a different layout, but you add text to it in the same way as the first slide.*

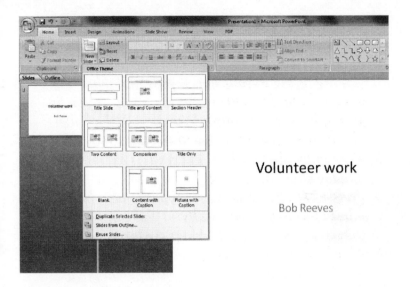

4 *Click where it says 'Click to add title' and type in the title for this slide. In this example 'Why volunteer?'*

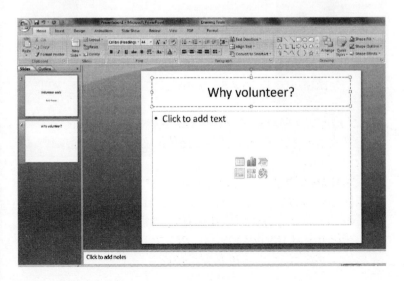

5 *Click where it says 'Click to add text'. You can now type in a series of bullet points. The idea of bullet points is that you summarize what it is you are trying to say. This means that what you write should be short and to the point. If you are presenting the slideshow, you can use the bullet points as prompts to what you want to say.*

6 *Type in the first bullet point. In this example 'Giving something back'.*

7 *Press ENTER. You will see that the next bullet point appears automatically so you can type in the next point. Type 'Helping the local community'.*

8 *Continue until you have made all the points you want to. In this example, there are five different points.*

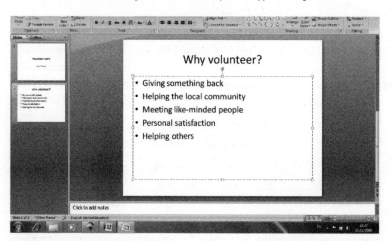

Hints and tips

The size of the font is automatic. If you type lots of bullet points, it will automatically make the font smaller to fit it all in.

27.4 Adding ClipArt to slides

Now we will add a slide with a picture in it. ClipArt is a library of images, some animated and some photographs. In the next example, there will be text and an image on the slide.

1 *Click on 'New Slide'.*
2 *Select the 'Title and Content' layout as before. The title and text can now be added in the same way that you added them in the previous slides.*
3 *In this example the slide title will be 'How to volunteer'.*
4 *The bullet list should read:*
   ▷ *Go to your nearest volunteer centre*
   ▷ *Look in Yellow Pages*
   ▷ *Volunteer online*
5 *Next add the image. Click on the 'Insert' tab and select 'ClipArt'.*
6 *The ClipArt library will be displayed on the right hand side. If you have worked through the chapters on Word and Publisher you will see that ClipArt works in exactly the same way here as it does in those programs.*
7 *ClipArt is organized in categories. The amount of images you have depends on what version of the software you have. You can search for a specific image by typing in key words. For example, if we wanted a ClipArt image of a computer, where it says 'Search for', type in 'computer' and press ENTER. Any images related to computers are now shown.*

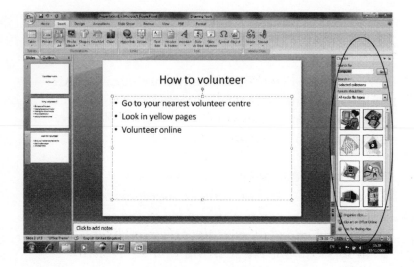

8 *In this case, it has found lots of suitable images. You may need to scroll down to see them all.*

9 *Double click on the image you want and it will be displayed on your slide. You can resize and move this in the usual way. Your finished slide will now look like this.*

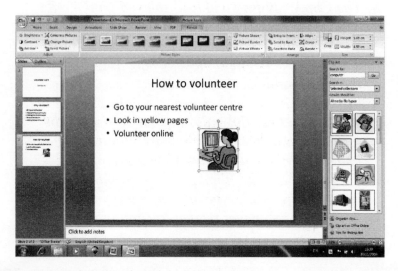

27.5 Adding photographs to slides

This section will show you how to insert a photograph. It assumes that you have already added some photographs onto your computer. If you have not done this yet, please see Chapters 17 to 19.

First, create a new slide into which to put the photograph:

1 *Add a new slide by clicking on 'New Slide' and selecting 'Title and Content' under the 'Home' tab. If you were creating a slideshow that was just photographs with no text, then you could choose the blank slide layout which is the last option.*
2 *Type in a title and the bullet point text in the usual way. In this example, the title is 'John: a case study'.*
3 *The bullet points should read:*
    ▷ *John volunteered at his local centre*
    ▷ *He volunteers one day a week*
    ▷ *He helps disabled people with their gardens*
    ▷ *He loves being outdoors and helping people*

Hints and tips

There is quite a lot of text for a smallish box here so you will see that PowerPoint automatically reduces the font size to fit it all in.

To add a photograph:

4 *Click on the 'Insert' tab from the options at the top.*
5 *Select 'Picture'. The Pictures folder is now shown. Assuming that your photograph is in this folder, find it in the list and double click on it.*
6 *The photograph will be inserted into the slide. The size of the photograph will depend on how the picture was saved – it may be the wrong size when you first insert it.*
7 *Click on the photograph.*
8 *Move the mouse pointer to one of the four corners until the pointer becomes a four-headed arrow.*
9 *Hold down the left mouse button and move the mouse – the photograph will re-size. When it is the size you want it, release the left mouse button.*

You can also move the picture around if you need to.

Hints and tips

You can also copy and paste images into PowerPoint. For example, if you found a good image on the Internet you could copy it from there and paste it into your slide.

27.6 Saving the slideshow

At this stage, it is worth saving the slideshow. The saving process is the same here as for all other software:

1 *Click on the 'Save' icon in the Quick Access toolbar, or select 'Save' after clicking on the Microsoft Office button.*
2 *Give your presentation a suitable name (e.g. Volunteer Work).*

27.7 Running the slideshow

When you run the slideshow, it will be shown as full-screen. This is how your audience will see it. They may be viewing it on their own computer, or you might be projecting it onto a big screen.

To view the slideshow:

1 *Press F5. The first slide is shown. Notice that it takes up the whole screen and that all of the menu options and taskbars have disappeared.*
2 *Click the mouse once. Slide 2 is now shown. Each click will move the slideshow on to the next slide until it reaches the end.*
3 *When you reach the end, right click and select 'End Show'.*
4 *You are taken back to the original view of your slideshow where you can make any further changes if you need to, or click on the cross to close PowerPoint.*

IMPORTANT THINGS TO REMEMBER FROM THIS CHAPTER

1 *You can use PowerPoint to create and show slideshows. These might contain text and pictures or perhaps a series of photographs.*

2 *Typically a slideshow is used as a visual aid to be shown while someone is talking, usually to a group.*

3 *Slideshows are made up of a series of slides each of which can contain text, graphics, photographs, video and sound.*

4 *There are different layouts for different purposes. For example, there is one that can be used for a title slide and another for text and images.*

5 *You will be working with large font sizes, which are designed to be shown to an audience and may be projected onto a big screen.*

6 *You can add as many slides as you like but as a rule of thumb you probably only need one slide for each minute you plan on talking.*

7 *It is common to use bullet points and then talk about the bullet points, rather than typing everything you want to say onto the slides.*

8 *You can add ClipArt to slides in the same way that you added them in Word and Publisher.*

9 *You can also add photographs in the same way.*

10 *When you run the slideshow it will take up the whole screen on your computer and you can click each time you want to move on to a new slide.*

Glossary

Chapters where the term is discussed are indicated by the bold numbers at the end of the definition.

address a way of identifying websites and emails (10)

address bar the place where you type in a web address e.g. www.hodder.co.uk when using Internet Explorer (8, 11)

address book an option in email software where you can store lists of email addresses (8)

adware malicious software that sets itself up on your computer when using the Internet (16)

aero flip 3D a way of viewing and selecting open windows from the desktop

attachment any file that is sent as well as an email, e.g. a photograph (9)

autorun any CD or DVD will play automatically when put in the computer (5)

autosum a formula (calculation) for adding a set of numbers in a spreadsheet (24)

backup a separate copy of your work usually saved onto a CD (20)

basket shows you what you have bought when you are shopping on the Internet (11)

blogging a diary on the Internet (15)

bold a way of making text stand out by making the text darker (6, 7)

bookmark a method of saving an Internet address so that you can go back to the page later; also known as 'Favourites' (10)

broadband high-speed access to the Internet (1, 13)

browse a method of looking through information (3, 11)

browser software for looking at and moving between websites (3, 10)

browsing the process of viewing web pages (12)

bullet a small dot at the beginning of a line of text – used to show a list of items (7, 27)

CD-R a CD that can have information saved to it once (2, 20)

CD-RW a CD that can have information saved to it over and over again (2, 20)

cell one small box in a spreadsheet (24)

chat room a place on a website where you can have online conversations with other people (13)

Clipart a library of drawn pictures or photographs that can be inserted into documents (7, 22, 27)

column used in spreadsheets to identify a collection of vertical cells; identified by a letter, e.g. column A (24)

computer system the generic term for a combination of the hardware (equipment) and software (programs) (1)

copy and paste a method of taking text or an image in one place and creating a copy of it somewhere else (7)

cursor the small line on the screen that shows you where the text will go when you start typing (6)

cut and paste a method of deleting text or an image from one place and putting it somewhere else (7)

database a collection of information on a related theme (26)

data type in database software, this describes what type of information is being stored, e.g. text or number (26)

dead link a hyperlink from a web page that does not lead to anything (10)

desktop the workspace in Windows – shows all the icons for the programs and folders on your computer; also, a type of computer that sits on the desk (as opposed to a laptop) (1)

download the process of getting something from the Internet onto your computer (3, 5)

drag holding down the left mouse button while moving the mouse (6, 7, 23)

DVD-R a disk that can have information saved to it once (2, 20)

DVD-RW a disk that can have information saved to it over and over again (2, 20)

eBay an online auction site (12)

email account a personal email address (8)

email provider a business that provides you will access to email, e.g. Yahoo!, BT, Tiscali, Microsoft (8)

field in a database, this refers to one items of information in a record (26)

file all information stored on the computer is stored in files, so a file could be a document, a slideshow, a photograph or any other kind of information (4, 6)

file name the name given to a file so that you know what it is (18)

file type indicates what type of information is stored in the file, e.g. a document, photographs, etc. (18)

file-sharing websites that allow you to share files (usually music or video) with other people – often illegally (16)

Filmstrip view a way of viewing files in Windows; particularly useful for looking at photographs (19)

filtering software that prevents certain websites from being viewed (16)

firewall a method of stopping hackers getting access to your computer when you are on the Internet (16)

flatbed scanner a device for copying printed documents and turning them into a computerized version (1, 3, 18)

floppy disk a device for storing information (20)

folder a place where files are stored on your computer e.g. My Documents (4)

folders tree a list of all of the folders that are on your computer (18)

font the style of text (6)

format the process of changing the way that something looks on the screen (6)

forum an online notice board where you can post messages and reply to others (13)

frame in desktop publishing software, this is a box that has text or pictures in it (22, 23)

gigabytes (GB) a measure of how much information can be stored on a computer (1)

gigahertz (Ghz) a measure of the speed of a processor, that is, how fast the computer works (1)

hacking where someone gains unauthorized access to your computer – usually when you are on the Internet (16)

hard disk a device inside the computer where all information is stored (18)

hardware all the physical parts of a computer (1, 5)

highlighted shows when a text or an image has been selected (6)

hits in a search engine, this shows the number of websites that are found when you type in some key words (10)

home page the first page of a website that usually contains an introduction to the website and lots of hyperlinks to other parts of the site (8)

hot key pressing certain combinations of keys as a quicker way of selecting certain options (6)

hyperlink a link from a web page that leads to other web pages (8, 10)

icons small pictures used to represent different things (4)

identity theft when someone pretends to be you with the intention of stealing from you (16)

inbox where messages are stored in email (8)

inkjet a type of printer that uses ink cartridges (1)

install the process of adding new software or hardware to the computer (5)

installation routine the process the computer goes through to add new software (5)

Internet a global connection of computers (8, 10)

IP address the unique number that is assigned to your computer when you are on the Internet (16)

iPod a device for storing and playing music with headphones (5)

iTunes software used for downloading and organizing music from the Internet (5)

jpg a file format for photographs and other images (9)

keywords the main words that you choose to type in when you are searching for something; usually refers to search engines on the Internet (10)

laptop a portable computer (1)

laser a type of printer (1)

left-aligned where text is lined up on the left-hand side (6)

link *see* hyperlink (8)

load the process of either installing software, or opening software on your computer (5)

log on the process of gaining access to a computer, or to websites; usually involves typing in a password (12, 13)

lookup wizard in databases, a way of creating a drop-down list (26)

mail merge the process of combining names and address stored in a database, with a standard letter (26)

media player software for playing music and video (5, 14)

megabytes (MB) a measure of how big the computer's memory is (1)

memory card a small plastic device inserted into a digital camera that stores the photographs (2)

memory stick a device that plugs into the computer and can be used for storing information (2, 20)

menu the words across the top of the screen in software that let you get at the various options (4)

Microsoft Office button found in the top left-hand corner of most Microsoft Office software, this gives you access to common options such as saving and printing (6, 7, 24, 25, 26, 27)

minimize closing a window but leaving it available in the Taskbar (4)

modem a device needed for connecting your computer to the Internet (1, 5)

mouse pointer the small arrow on the screen that can be controlled by moving the mouse (4, 10)

multimedia anything that combines text, graphics, sound and video (14)

newsgroup a way of posting and reading messages on the Internet – organized into topics (13)

numbered point a way of creating a list with a number in front of each item (7)

online refers to being on the Internet (5, 11)

online banking doing your banking on the Internet (15)

operating system software needed to make your computer work e.g. Windows 7 (1)

password a way of ensuring the correct person is using the computer (8, 16)

PayPal a method of paying for something that you have bought over the Internet (12, 16)

peripheral any piece of equipment that can be used in conjunction with your computer, e.g. a printer or scanner (2)

phishing where someone tries to get your bank account details from you via email, so that they can steal from you (16)

player *see* media player (14)

point size refers to the size of the font (text) (6)

port a socket on your computer where something can be plugged in (17)

portal a website that provides links to other websites of a similar topic (15)

premium dialer malicious software that connects your computer to the Internet at £1.50 or more each minute (16)

preview a way of looking at something on the computer before carrying out an action (4, 18)

print preview a way of looking at something on the computer before printing (6, 7)

Quick Access toolbar found in the top left-hand corner just next to the Microsoft Office button in most Microsoft Office software, this gives you access to common options such as saving and printing (6, 7, 24, 25, 26, 27)

record in database software, refers to all the information stored about one person, or object (26)

repeat will put back anything that you have just undone using the 'undo' option (7)

resolution the clarity of an image either on screen or printed (2, 18)

restart switching the computer off and on again (5)

restore making a window bigger or smaller (4)

right-aligned lining up text on the right (6)

row in spreadsheets, refers to each horizontal set of cells (24)

scanner *see* flatbed scanner (1)

scroll bar the method used to move up and down a page (6)

scroll down moving down a page (8)

scrolling the process of moving up, down or across a page (7)

search a method of finding specific information when using the computer (7, 11, 12, 27)

search engine software for searching the Internet (10)

secure site a website that has extra protection for people making online purchases (10, 16)

shortcut an icon, usually on the desktop that opens a program or folder (4, 5)

shut down the process of switching the computer off (4)

slideshow a way of presenting information to others on the computer (4, 27)

social networking websites where you can display a personal profile, meet other people and keep in touch with them

software the programs that run on computers, e.g. Windows, Word, etc. (1, 5)

sort in databases, or spreadsheets, a method of sequencing information (27)

spam the email equivalent of junk mail (8)

spell-checker automatic checking of spellings (6)

spreadsheet software for handling numerical information (3, 25)

spyware bad software that installs itself on your computer when you are on the Internet (16)

start-up routine the process that your computer goes through when you switch it on (4)

storage devices any device used for storing information, e.g. CD, DVD, memory stick (2)

subfolder a folder within a folder; used to store files (19)

tabs a method of selecting different options in Word, Excel, Access and Powerpoint. Tabs appear across the top of the screen in each of these programs. (6, 7, 24, 25, 26, 27)

Taskbar the small bar at the bottom of the screen that shows what programs, folders and files are currently open (4, 20)

text wrapping the way that text will automatically move down to the next line when it runs out of space (6, 22)

thread a topic of discussion in a newsgroup (13)

thumbnail a way of viewing files as a small image – particularly useful for looking through photographs (9, 17)

toolbar a collection of icons in a program; an alternative to using the menus (4)

undo undoes whatever you did last (7)

updates additions to software that provide new features (3)

uploading the process of putting information onto the Internet; can refer to the process of putting information onto your computer, including digital images from a camera (17)

USB a method for connecting devices to your computer (1, 2)

USB port the socket on the front or back of the computer where you plug in a USB device (1, 2, 20)

user name/user ID required for some Internet services along with a password so that you can access them (12, 16)

virus malicious software that installs itself and can cause damage to your computer (3, 16, 20)

virus checker software that prevents viruses damaging your computer (3, 9)

VOIP Voice over Internet Protocol – allows you to make telephone calls over the Internet using your computer (13)

web page a page of information on the Internet (10)

web-based a service that is provided over the Internet (3, 8)

website several pages of information on the Internet (7, 10)

Windows desktop see desktop (4)

Wizard a selection of screens that guide you through a particular process (5, 21)

WordArt a way of creating artistic effects with text, available in all Microsoft software (23)

word processing software for typing and creating documents (6, 7)

World Wide Web the collective name for all the websites and (www) web pages on the Internet (10)

worm *see* virus (16)

wrap *see* text wrapping (6)

wrapping *see* text wrapping (25)

Index

Credits